# Strategic Leadership of Portfolio and Project Management

# Strategic Leadership of Portfolio and Project Management

Timothy J. Kloppenborg and Laurence J. Laning

First published in 2012 by
Business Expert Press, LLC
222 East 46th Street, New York, NY 10017
www.businessexpertpress.com

ISBN-13: 978-1-60649-294-9 (paperback)

ISBN-13: 978-1-60649-295-6 (e-book)

DOI 10.4128/ 9781606492956

Business Expert Press Supply and Operations Management collection

Collection ISSN: 2156-8189 (print)
Collection ISSN: 2156-8200 (electronic)

Cover design by Jonathan Pennell
Interior design by Exeter Premedia Services Private Ltd., Chennai, India

First edition: 2012

10 9 8 7 6 5 4 3 2 1

Printed in the United States of America.

# Abstract

This book is aimed at executive leaders of organizations. Leaders from all organizations will benefit from this book, but especially organizations that may have limited resources and bench strength. This book instructs executive leadership teams on implementing strategy through identifying, selecting, prioritizing, resourcing, and governing an optimal combination of projects and other work. This book also tells executives who serve as a sponsor or who have a project manager direct report what they need to do at each project stage. Advice is given to the executive who owns the project management competency for the company on utilizing input from customers, employees, and processes. Much of the organization's work is dependent on information technology, and understanding and using information technology as a strategic weapon helps an organization become competitive and effectively implement their business strategies. All of these portfolio and project decisions need to be made based upon both qualitative and quantitative data using reliable analysis methods.

# Keywords

strategy, execution, portfolio management, executive sponsorship, executive leadership, project management, information technology, data-based decision making, organizational assessment

# Contents

*Preface* ............................................................................................................ix

Chapter 1   Implementing Strategy Through
               Portfolios and Projects .........................................................1

Chapter 2   Managing a Portfolio to Implement Strategy:
               A Leadership Team Role ......................................................17

Chapter 3   Sponsoring Successful Projects ..........................................43

Chapter 4   Leading Project Managers:
               The Project Executive Role ..................................................75

Chapter 5   Listening to Customers, Employees, and Processes:
               A Chief Projects Officer's Role ..........................................109

Chapter 6   Understanding Information Technology
               Opportunities and Challenges:
               A Chief Information Officer's Role ....................................137

Chapter 7   Making Sensible Decisions Using Data:
               A Responsibility of All Executives ....................................177

Chapter 8   Conclusions .....................................................................215

*Notes*..............................................................................................................221

*References* .......................................................................................................225

*Index* .............................................................................................................231

# Preface

We met over 20 years ago. Laurie was midcareer at Procter & Gamble (P&G) having other work experience and his PhD. Tim was untenured at Xavier having a few years of business and military experience. At the time, we were part of a team redesigning the MBA program at Xavier. Since then, Laurie has held roles of increasing responsibility during a 28-year career at P&G including introducing data management, leading the implementation of SAP in the supply chain, applying information technology to P&G's new product innovation process, and retiring as the chief information technology enterprise architect. Tim finished his U.S. Air Force Reserve career with transportation, procurement, and quality assurance assignments, worked his way up to distinguished professor at Xavier, wrote nearly 100 publications including several books, consulted and trained with many clients, and supervised many student teams who helped nonprofit organizations.

With our combined 70 years of corporate, academic, military, consulting, training, board, and volunteer experience, we have had many discussions concerning the common challenges in all of those organizations. One central challenge is when different parts of the organization either do not understand other parts or are even working at cross-purposes. We have combined our leadership, quality, project, information technology, and decision sciences backgrounds to create a short volume with the intent of addressing challenges that are common to many organizations. This book applies the Pareto Principle—that is, choosing the 20% of ideas and techniques that will provide 80% of the value to leaders.

# CHAPTER 1

# Implementing Strategy Through Portfolios and Projects

This book, *Strategic Leadership of Portfolio and Project Management,* provides an approach to leadership by linking strategy to the action necessary to successfully implement it. Many companies face varying strategic implementation challenges as can be seen in Table 1.1.

The book guides executives through strategic implementation by creating a framework of key concepts and tools from portfolio management, executive sponsorship, project management, quality, information

*Table 1.1. Strategic Implementation Challenges Facing Companies*

| Company | Challenge |
|---|---|
| Duke Energy is one of the largest electric utility companies in the United States. | Duke continually faced large uncertainties in regulatory and business conditions and a huge pipeline of needs. |
| TriHealth consists of several large hospitals, physician groups, and related health-care facilities. | TriHealth did not have consistency in executive leadership roles, especially for projects. |
| Messer is a full-service commercial construction company specializing in health care, higher education, and life sciences. | Messer needed consistently successful construction projects. |
| The Midland Company delivers specialized insurance services for mobile homes, classic cars, motorcycles, and snowmobiles. | Midland has many methodologies and needed to decide how they can help execute the key initiatives of its business strategy. |
| YourEncore is a consulting company with a network of veteran scientific, engineering, and technical experts. | YourEncore needed to determine whether its information technology systems would be strong enough to support future growth. |
| Givaudan is a global leader in the fragrance and flavor industries. | Givaudan needed to make decisions about what development projects to undertake. |

technology (IT), and decision-making. Each chapter describes how one of these companies met its implementation challenge by using concepts from that chapter.

The scope of this book encompasses both ongoing operational work and projects. This is a book about holistically leading an organization to achieve success as defined by four sets of competing objectives that are explained below. This chapter starts by describing the four sets of competing objectives faced by most organizations. Then projects are defined including how each proceeds through a life cycle and how success is determined. The need for standards and the roles executives perform in leading an organization's portfolio of projects are introduced. The chapter concludes with an overview of the other chapters in this book.

## Competing Objectives

In many organizations, executives determine strategy and managers implement it. Often a gap can exist in successfully accomplishing both objectives. Organizations also frequently struggle with successfully accomplishing three other sets of competing objectives: sustainable organizational capability and current business results, project goals and operational goals, and competing goals of different organizational functions. Successful organizations consistently deliver each set of these competing objectives. This book is aimed to help you simultaneously better achieve each of these sets of competing objectives by describing concepts and tools for implementing strategy through carefully identified, aligned, selected, prioritized, resourced, and controlled projects.

### Executives Set Strategy and Managers Implement It

Executives often do not get very involved with projects. This may be due to excessive demands upon their time. Lack of executive involvement could also be due to lack of understanding of the technical nature of some of the project work or fear that if they are seen as closely tied to a project, they may be held responsible for any failure. Limited executive involvement in project implementation can lead to a gap between the executive level that develops strategy and the management level that is charged with implementing it.

Among the reasons for the failure of strategic plan implementations are the leadership's imperfect:

- understanding of customers' true needs and wants,
- estimation of resource competence,
- coordination of work,
- ability to secure commitment from both senior management and employees,
- creation of and adherence to logical plans,
- communication with employees and other stakeholders, and
- ability to identify and manage risks.[1]

## Organizational Capability and Business Results

In this book, we describe how companies strive to simultaneously achieve improvements in organizational capability and desired business results as stated by organizational objectives. Often the pressure to achieve impressive short-term business results can lead to decisions that do not promote long-term organizational capability. Organizational capability can be expressed in terms of a company's:

- human resources: its number, quality, skills, and experience;
- physical and material resources: machines, land, buildings;
- financial resources: money and credit;
- information resources: pool of knowledge, databases;
- intellectual resources: copyrights, designs, patents, and so forth.[2]

## Project Goals and Operational Goals

Yet another gap may exist between the project and the operational types of work in an organization, as shown in Figure 1.1. Operations (shown as processes in Figure 1.1) typically are the mechanism by which knowledge is turned into revenue. Thus, it is very important to keep this work

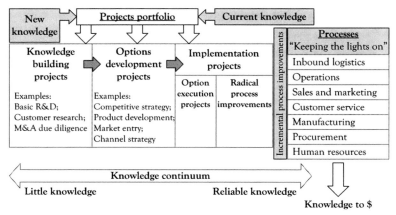

*Figure 1.1. Intertwining of projects and processes to create sustainable value.*

moving effectively as the cash generated by these processes is the lifeblood that sustains an organization. The firm needs knowledge to successfully capitalize upon and this is where projects come in handy. Projects of various types create knowledge ranging from early stage research to specifically applied process improvements. Without the knowledge an organization gains from such work, it would quickly become obsolete.[3]

### Competing Goals of Different Organizational Functions

Another set of competing objectives occurs between functional "silos" of organizations. Each functional area of an organization has work to accomplish. An overemphasis on one department can shortchange another. Coordination between departments needs to be consciously developed through effective communication and cultural change.

In this book, we describe how leaders strive to accomplish all four sets of competing objectives. Leaders can coordinate efforts at both the executive and the managerial levels. When leaders bridge the executive–manager gap, they better deliver both current business results and organizational capability improvements. They also develop and capitalize upon knowledge with projects and processes, and coordinate various department goals. All these things can be enhanced by effectively identifying, aligning, selecting, prioritizing, resourcing, and controlling a best portfolio of project and operational work to achieve all of the organizational objectives.

# Projects

A project is a temporary endeavor undertaken to create a unique product, service, or result.[4] Because it is temporary, each project goes through a predictable series of stages called a life cycle. Because it is an endeavor, each project requires resources to complete. Because it is unique, each project requires planning and control in a variety of areas such as scope (the amount of work), risk, budgeting, and so forth. Because projects create products, services, or results, stakeholders exist who are counting on those deliverables. Those stakeholders must be identified, understood, prioritized, communicated with, and satisfied.

## Universality of Projects

In many ways, the world is changing faster than ever due to globalization, IT, and knowledge creation. Project management can be a great way to plan and manage changes proactively. Project management skills enable people to quickly and flexibly plan and deliver a wide variety of projects. A few of the most useful skills are:

- initiating the effort with a charter,
- developing communication plans and dealing effectively with stakeholders,
- dividing work into manageable portions,
- scheduling complex interrelated work,
- managing risks and change, and
- reporting progress.

Work in any functional arena can be modeled and managed as a project. Project Management Institute (PMI) is the leading global professional group that deals with project management. With over 370,000 members, PMI has communities of interest in dozens of industries, plus various functional groups including financial services, human resources, information systems, leadership, retail, and transportation.[5]

Project management techniques can be applied to an endeavor of any size, from a very simple endeavor to a highly involved one. Even for the simplest projects, it is important to be able to state what will be accomplished and why it is important to the organization. The largest and most complicated projects share the need of starting with what will be accomplished and why, but the level of detail in planning and managing them should be commensurate with the challenge.

### Project Leadership Roles

A variety of executive leadership responsibilities concerning projects need to be fulfilled if a company is to optimally implement its strategy. Who handles each of these responsibilities and what their titles are varies considerably from one company to another. For clarity, we will use consistent titles for the roles we describe.

We need to clarify a few things about these roles. Some of the responsibilities can be delegated from an executive to a manager, whereas others should be retained. In larger organizations, sometimes several people each have a portion of the duties we describe in a given role. In smaller organizations, one person may have more than one of these roles and other responsibilities also.

We have two general pieces of advice regarding these executive roles. First, since their duties are so different, do not use the same person in the role of a sponsor and a project manager on the same project. Second, ensure you understand each role and the reason for it. Make the conscious decision to have someone perform each duty.

Identifying these leadership roles in your company is helpful in assigning the right person to perform each duty, thereby ensuring all responsibilities are performed and helping executives understand where they can improve. The executive roles we use in this book are leadership team, sponsor, project executive, chief projects officer (CPO), and chief information officer (CIO).

A **leadership team** is responsible for the results of all work in the portfolio. This team is often composed of the top person in the organization and the people who report to them. The people described in some or all of the other roles may be members of the leadership team. They collectively make portfolio decisions of identifying, selecting, prioritizing, resourcing, and governing projects.

A **sponsor** wants the project results and is jointly responsible for achieving them along with the project executive and the project manager. She is the key decision-maker for the project. The sponsor provides overall project resources, oversees stakeholders, and delivers project results according to the business case. The sponsor has specific responsibilities during each stage of the project life cycle. If the project manager normally reports to the sponsor, she will also serve as the project executive.

A **project executive** supervises one or more project managers who report directly to them and is jointly responsible for delivering project results with the sponsor and the project manager. He provides functional resources, governs methods used on the project, helps the project manager develop leadership competency, and delivers project results according to plan. The project executive has specific task and coaching responsibilities at each stage in the project life cycle. The project executive may also be the sponsor.

A **CPO** responsible for developing project management competency and facilitating the leadership team as they make portfolio decisions. The CPO has ongoing responsibilities in developing the project management system and competence along with specific facilitating duties at key portfolio decision points.

A **CIO** is responsible for all the IT needs of the company. The CIO works with senior management to define a strategic IT master plan that implements business strategy. The CIO deals extensively with internal resources along with IT consultants and IT vendor companies.

We describe each of these roles in more detail in the following chapters. The role of the sponsor is the only executive role that is clearly defined in professional standards. We use those standards and add to them based upon our research over the last five years concerning specific duties and the impact each has on various measures of project success.

While this book is written for executives, we will refer to the following three project management roles. First, the project manager is the focal point and is responsible for project planning, communications, and implementation. The second role is the project core team. This team is comprised of members who are involved in the project for the entire duration and who help the project manager make decisions and carry out tasks. The third role is that of subject matter experts who are extra hands brought on the project as needed.

## *Project Success*

Project success has been widely studied and many researchers have proposed overlapping suggestions of how to measure it. At one time, many people viewed project success narrowly as delivering to specification, on time, and within budget. During the 21st century, many people have dramatically expanded their views on project success. One way of incorporating the many suggestions of project success into a useful framework is to group the measures into (1) project management success, (2) business results achieved, and (3) operational capability improvements.

Project Success Measurements

1. Project management success
   - Specifications
   - Cost
   - Schedule.
2. Business results achieved
   - Profit
   - Market share
   - Increased sales
   - New product
   - Customer satisfaction.
3. Organizational capability improvements
   - Improved customer capability
   - Sustainable results
   - Team member loyalty
   - Team member development
   - Team member satisfaction

- Organizational learning
- New technology and methods.[6]

Project management success means delivering exactly what you promised on time and within budget. This is important, but far from the total understanding of project success. Projects also contribute toward current business results with sales, profits, products, and satisfied customers. Projects can further be envisioned as a means of improving the organizational capabilities of the customer's and the parent organization's technologies and people.

Current research from various industries and project types consistently shows satisfying customers is the most important success criterion and if that is accomplished, many of the other business results and organizational capability improvement measures will be realized.[7] However, satisfying the customer completely and achieving the project management success measures of on time, within budget, and to specification do not always go together without good project planning and execution.

## Project Life Cycle

Most researchers and practicing managers use a stage-gate or life cycle model (Figure 1.2) to understand how projects vary from one point in time to another. The concept of a project life cycle is that during a given stage certain requirements must be met or the project is not allowed to pass to the next stage. Many industries have their own specific life cycle models due to the specific characteristics projects encounter. For example, construction projects have very different demands than research and development projects.

Despite the uniqueness of specific industries, many people use a generic project life cycle model as a starting point. The most basic model often includes some sort of initiation to make the project official followed by other stages to plan, execute, and close the project. Project responsibilities start even before the initiation stage with selection of the project. Responsibilities also extend after project completion to ensure the promised benefits are realized. For this book, we use the model in Figure 1.2

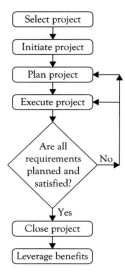

*Figure 1.2. The project life cycle model.*

to describe how responsibilities change from one stage to the next. If all of the work is not accomplished, the flow of the project work either returns to planning or continues to the execution stage. For many projects, it is impractical to plan the entire project at the outset; it makes more sense to plan and accomplish some work to being with and use the results of the early work to help plan future work.

## The Need for Standards

Throughout this book, you will see the topic of standards dealt with in specific examples. Here, we talk about the topic of standards in general as it applies across the board.

The simple question is, why should we have standards and what benefits do they provide? Clearly, there are processes in your organization where you want creativity and innovation to prevail. But there are also many processes where doing things differently or not in the same manner each time provides no benefits and simply costs you money. Having a standard way of doing things in these types of processes makes a lot of sense.

Example processes for which organizations would prefer to have a standard way of doing things consistently across the entire organization are:

- preparing and approving expense reports for business travel,
- processing financial transactions,
- taking orders from "customers,"
- a stage-gate process for new product and service development,
- reserving conference rooms, and
- having a common methodology for managing projects, and so forth.

The above list could go on. Note there are both internally and externally developed standards. An internally developed standard involves adopting your best practice to how a common process is best executed and then reapplying that approach as your standard for this process. The expense report example above could be such an internal standard. Adopting an externally developed standard, as the name implies, involves researching and selecting a standard that has been developed by a professional organization or a vendor. A common example is adopting the PMI project management methodology for managing projects.

The primary benefits of adopting standards are:

- Standards allow you to leverage scale. If you have operations in multiple locations, your people only have to learn one way to implement the process.
- Standards also provide a common vocabulary and experience for your people as they relate to the standardized processes.
- For processes where you use automated/computerized tools, using standards means you can have a single tool to buy and support.
- In the case of adopting externally developed standards, you clearly benefit from the experience of many people's use of this standard in many different types of organizations.

## One Size May Not Fit All

While in many situations standardizing to a single approach may be beneficial, there are instances where having one standard will not meet the needs of the widely varying work processes in varying businesses, markets, or cultures. An example one of the authors (Laning) is in the 1990s when Procter & Gamble (P&G) chose to implement the Systems, Applications, and Products (SAP) software in  its global supply chains. The initial rollout of global SAP solutions often had a single configuration/version. We found that having only one standard process for supply chain processes was too restrictive and added unnecessary costs due to the adoption of a single solution that provided much more functionality than needed in small, simple manufacturing plants. Subsequently, many supply chain processes at P&G moved to have three types of solutions (e.g., small, medium, and large) versus having only one solution. This allowed the establishment of standards and the realization of cost benefits in addition to enabling the option of having solutions that were appropriate for the different business situations based on the differences in their complexity. This allowed the standards to take into consideration factors such as size and complexity of a manufacturing plant, whether the business was regulated or nonregulated, and how many SAP modules were being implemented in that business. Therefore, in some situations that vary widely in terms of size and complexity, having a few clearly defined standards versus having only one standard may provide great benefits.

## Fostering Creativity Through Control

A standard approach is like rules and boundaries in a game. All teams play on the same court and follow the same rules. Understanding the limits these rules and boundaries impose allows a coach to develop different strategies based on the skills of his players and the challenges posed by a given opponent. Likewise, standards are like rules and boundaries that help everyone understand the normal limits and grant thoughtful leaders the chance to use innovative approaches within those limits.

# Chapter Overviews

The next six chapters describe conceptual knowledge and demonstrate skills executives will find useful in simultaneously achieving each of the four sets of competing objectives. Each chapter introduction will include the purpose of the chapter, a dilemma faced by the company chosen to demonstrate the chapter concepts, and the key question the chapter answers. The body of each chapter varies considerably with some including more concepts and others including more techniques. Each chapter ends with what the chosen company did to solve its dilemma, a summary of how the chapter contributes to enhancing the achievement of the dual sets of objectives, and a set of the top 10 assessment questions executives can use to determine how well their company is currently performing.

The assessment questions in each chapter are a unique feature of this book. Their intent is to highlight the key areas the authors believe you need to think about and evaluate for your organization. If this book is used in an academic setting, the assessment questions can be used to assess a student's knowledge of an area.

Figure 1.3 summarizes the book at a glance.

Chapter 2 describes a work portfolio as the entire body of work an organization is doing to best accomplish its goals, subject to the limits of resources and its tolerance for risk. Then the components of portfolio management are described and a method for accomplishing them

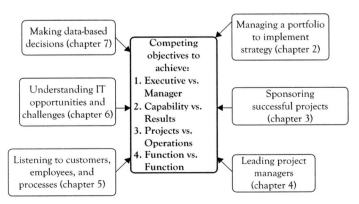

*Figure 1.3. Overview of the book.*

is detailed. The components include identifying, selecting, prioritizing, resourcing, and governing the organization's work. The leadership team often collectively makes the portfolio decisions.

Chapter 3 defines the role an executive serving as a sponsor when she wants a manager and a team to lead a project that will create something she values. The overarching responsibilities of a sponsor are to provide resources, oversee stakeholders, and deliver results. The chapter also details the few select behaviors busy executive sponsors can perform at each stage of a project to enhance the probability of project success.

Chapter 4 describes the role of the project executive—that is, directly supervising a project manager. The responsibilities of a project manager are described so that an executive can understand the different roles a project manager plays compared with the roles played by a functional manager. The remainder of the chapter deals with specific task and coaching responsibilities of a project executive at each stage of the project life cycle.

Chapter 5 describes how the CPO can use quality approaches when implementing strategy through projects. These concepts guide an executive who is responsible for developing project management competency and facilitate the leadership team as they make portfolio decisions. This executive needs to incorporate input from customers, employees, and processes.

Chapter 6 explains the basics of what IT is and what it makes possible. The chapter also shows how the CIO works with other executives to define a strategic IT master plan that implements the business strategy. The chapter concludes with best practices on when and how to use IT consultants and IT vendor companies.

Chapter 7 makes the case for the analysis of both quantitative and qualitative data in making decisions within your organization. The chapter provides guidance to all executives regarding how to define and collect clean and useful data. The chapter then concisely takes you through a careful selection of simple yet powerful analysis techniques to use within your organization to make better decisions that have more impact.

Chapter 8 highlights the key learnings we want you to take away from each chapter. We then give you specific ideas of how to apply what you have learned in a call to action for your organization.

The appendixes in this book are intended for readers who need to master the fundamentals of an area and do not have sufficient knowledge or experience in the area. For example, Appendix B is intended for readers who have little understanding of the basics of IT and need to get up to speed on topics such as hardware, software, telecommunications, and databases. Appendixes are included in chapters 5, 6, and 7.

# CHAPTER 2

# Managing a Portfolio to Implement Strategy: A Leadership Team Role

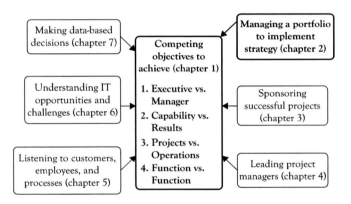

## Executive Leadership Team

Making decisions about the work portfolio of a company is the responsibility of the executive leadership team. The leadership team is generally the top person and his or her direct reports. The leadership team should collectively represent or at least understand all facets of the business so decision impacts can be understood. They set the overall priorities based upon the firm's strategy. In small organizations there is often one leadership team. In large organizations there may be leadership teams at both the corporate level and at lower levels. In some complex organizations one leadership team is used to select, prioritize, and resource projects while huge projects will have their own leadership teams (sometimes called boards) to govern them.

Sponsors, project executives, chief project officers (CPO), and chief information officers (CIO) described in the next four chapters of this book are often members of the leadership team. The leadership team often has a person who facilitates their work. In this book, we will call that person the CPO.

In this book, we will discuss the role of the leadership team regardless of whether there are one or multiple teams. The leadership team develops, manages, uses, and improves the portfolio system described in this chapter. Some leadership teams also resource projects, at least in part. It is common for the leadership team to select at least the sponsor for each project. Other leadership teams select project managers (although the selected sponsor frequently has a large say in choice of project manager). Some leadership teams will even decide what scarce individuals such as key technical leads get assigned to each project.

Most organizations would prefer to undertake far more work than they have resources to commit. This chapter describes how to select the set of projects and other work that collectively best help an organization reach its goals. The purpose of this chapter is to help you:

- articulate what a work portfolio is and why you need to consciously develop one;
- determine how many projects and at what level of complexity your company is capable of performing;
- develop criteria for selecting and prioritizing work;
- help everyone in your organization identify potential projects that will enable you to reach your goals;
- work with your leadership team to select and prioritize the portfolio of projects that best meet your strategic goals;
- begin new projects only when you have the necessary resources; and
- exercise just enough control to ensure the projects are successful.

## Duke Energy Case to Utilize a Work Portfolio

By any measure, Duke Energy is one of the largest electric utilities in the United States. Duke's core electric Transmission and Distribution business comprises over $50 billion in power delivery assets providing energy to 7.1 million customers throughout a 104,000 square mile

*(Continued)*

land area in six different states. Accurately identifying, prioritizing, and executing the continuous stream of projects subject to capital investment limits are the foundation of the Duke's ability to meet its strategic objectives.

Duke's management team recognized that the following concepts are essential to the success of the budgeting and project selection process...

- incorporate the organization's current strategy, sustainability objectives, and corporate values;
- be well-understood, communicated, and accepted throughout the organization;
- ensure consistency across all geographic areas to withstand regulatory scrutiny and provide rationale to substantiate decisions open to public opinion;
- provide a clear indication to decision-makers of the value and risk associated with undertaking or forgoing each project investment;
- produce certainty over an extended time horizon regarding the spend strategy, work plan, and associated resource requirements while enabling flexibility to adjust to business conditions; and
- assume that selected and ongoing projects will be managed as a portfolio allowing individual project dynamics to be absorbed by the strength and diversity of the portfolio.

**The key question Duke Energy Leaders faced** is how they could develop a project portfolio system dynamic enough for them to identify, select, prioritize resource, and govern a portfolio of projects that will best help them achieve their objectives in the face of uncertain business conditions. This is the classic portfolio question and the subject of this chapter.

## Portfolio Management Defined

Perhaps the best way to understand portfolio management is to first consider a financial portfolio. If a person manages his own retirement account, advice is usually given to diversify. The primary reason to diversify is to reach financial goals while reducing risk to an acceptable level. Place some investments in stock funds or indexes, some in bonds, perhaps some in real estate or near cash instruments. The money in stocks and bonds is diversified by industry and geography. One further portion of the normal financial advice is to periodically review the portfolio to ensure it is still balanced in a sensible manner considering the current conditions. Recommendations like these are given so that a person can achieve his financial goals without taking on too much risk.

The work of a company can likewise be considered as a portfolio. The company will have goals to accomplish. Some of the goals will be financial. Others will be determined through strategic planning. The company will want to achieve these goals without taking on too much risk. The way to accomplish this is to consider each portion of work the company undertakes as an investment. The company will invest managerial effort, employee time, and a variety of resources—financial and other—into each work activity in hopes of securing a desired output.

### Project Management Institute (PMI)

PMI is the world's largest professional organization that is dedicated specifically to project and portfolio management issues several standards that define portfolios and their management.

A **portfolio** is "a collection of projects and other work that are grouped together to facilitate effective management of that work to meet strategic business objectives. The components of a portfolio are quantifiable: they can be measured, ranked, and prioritized."[1]

One definition of **portfolio management** is "the coordinated management of portfolio components to achieve organizational objectives... Portfolio management uses tools... to identify, select, prioritize, govern, monitor, and report the contributions of the components to, and their relative alignment with, organizational objectives... The goal of portfolio management is to ensure the organization is doing the right work rather than doing work right."[2]

A second, complementary definition of **portfolio management** from PMI is "the centralized management of one or more portfolios to include: identifying, prioritizing, authorizing, managing and controlling projects and other work to achieve strategic business objectives. The organization's strategic plan and available resources guide the investments. An ongoing interaction of work is needed to maintain a balanced portfolio."[3]

### PRojects IN Controlled Environments (PRINCE2)

PRINCE2 is the standard for project management in the United Kingdom, providing guidance both to organizational leaders as they manage organizational systems and direct managers who, in turn, manage projects.

A **portfolio** is "all the programmes and stand-alone projects being undertaken by an organization. **Portfolio management** includes ensuring each potential project meets a business need and provides value; tolerances are defined for each project objective to establish limits of delegated authority; and an executive is responsible for ensuring each project is focused on achieving its objectives."[4]

### Applied Portfolio Definitions Used In this Book

A work portfolio typically includes both routine work of producing products and services and "keeping the lights on" along with nonroutine work of projects. By considering all work at a company as part of a portfolio, the leaders need to explicitly determine how many of their resources (human, financial, and other) will be allocated to each type of work. Some projects are to create or improve work processes, products, or services. Other projects exist to implement changes. Similar to a financial portfolio, most firms would expect to diversify their work into each of these classes. Even within a class—such as projects for implementing change—a firm would typically diversify. A company may decide to have one major change initiative such as implementing an enterprise resource management system along with various small changes at the same time. The company, however, would probably not elect to start two huge changes at the same time.

We choose to emphasize certain parts of portfolio management in our task list for executives. The goal of portfolio management is to achieve the maximum benefit toward the strategic goals of a company. To accomplish this, executives need to identify, select, prioritize, resource, and govern an appropriate portfolio of projects and other work.

*Figure 2.1. Portfolio management to implement strategy.*

Portfolio management is an outgrowth of strategy development. It is the successful execution of that strategy. It precedes and exerts control over project management as shown in Figure 2.1.

Organizations optimize competitive advantage by reaping better returns on their investments than their competitors. Portfolio management is vital as by its very design it helps an organization select a set of work the leaders believe will achieve the organization's goals, subject to constraints of time, money, and other resources. Portfolio management provides a good return on investment (ROI) since the ideal set of work is being performed and managed. By carefully selecting and controlling the work, executives strive to perform at a high ethical standard. It is emotionally satisfying to the workers as they know the work they are doing is critical to the organization and why.

## Components of Portfolio Management

In the section below, we introduce each of the executive tasks of identifying, selecting, prioritizing, resourcing, and governing work. Later, we demonstrate an easy, spreadsheet technique to perform them.

### Identifying Potential Projects

Identifying projects starts with leaders of an organization assessing the types and sizes of projects they are capable of performing. It makes no sense to encourage workers to propose projects that the organization is not capable of performing. Stretch goals are fine—but be somewhat realistic.

Executives determine strategic directions. If this identification has no focus, much time and many irrelevant ideas may be considered. The strategic goals of the company can be used to guide this identification. For instance, Duke Energy (in the chapter example) leaders clearly and consistently communicate their company's current strategy, sustainability objectives, corporate values, and value-risk assessment factors so all parts of the company can propose projects. Many companies will update their strategic plan every year and have some consistency along with some changes from year to year.

Identifying projects involves everyone in the organization. Hands-on workers can identify potential improvements in work methods. Sales people can identify potential market opportunities. Some of the projects identified will be to improve the organization's capabilities and others will be to deliver current business results.

Strengths, Weaknesses, Opportunities, and Threats (SWOT) analysis can be another method for identifying potential projects. This framework forces a company's leaders to consider internal strengths and weaknesses and external opportunities and threats. It is more strategic than just asking all associates to suggest improvements within their sphere of work. Another advantage of SWOT analysis is it explicitly considers risk. Internal weaknesses and external threats pose risks. Remember, a work portfolio is designed to help a company achieve as much toward its goals as possible, but only at an acceptable risk level. The two methods can be used together. All workers can make suggestions to their managers and SWOT analysis can consider all of the ideas as input.

### Selecting Projects and Other Work

Selecting projects is a critical role for the leaders of an organization. Organizational capability is built through projects. Projects are used to develop new products and processes, institute organizational changes, as well as to improve existing products and processes. However, a work portfolio also consists of performing ongoing processes "keeping the lights on." One way to envision the sum of an organization's work portfolio is to describe work as projects to create knowledge and managing processes to capitalize upon that knowledge as shown in chapter 1. Ideally a variety of projects of each type will be selected so the organization continues to improve while making the necessary profit.

## Prioritizing Projects and Other Work

Once the projects and ongoing process work are selected for a fiscal year or fiscal quarter, the next questions are—what do we do first and how do we settle conflicts? The answer to both is the work needs to be prioritized. It is tempting to say yes to worthwhile work (at either an organizational or a personal level), but difficult to say no. By prioritizing, one is not saying no to the work that is not quite as important or urgent, but is saying other work must proceed first. Psychologically this is helpful, as it does not mean you need to say no to someone. Rather you can say "help us get this most urgent work done first and then we will have the ability to do your project the right way."

Both research and practice have consistently shown that the way to accomplish the most work over a period of time is to start less work at a time, work hard to accomplish the work quickly, and then start other work. This is more efficient than extensive multitasking, which forces a person to frequently change over from one task to another. The more complicated a project is, the more time it takes to mentally remember where one was when interrupted. This goes against the grain of current practice in many organizations where people who work on many things simultaneously are valued. Remember, the goal is to accomplish more of the work that helps an organization achieve goals over a period of time, not how many things a person can juggle at one point in time.

## Resourcing Projects and Other Work

One of the classic problems in many organizations is that when necessary work comes along, executives tell their managers and workers to do it without consideration for how much work they are already engaged in. This forces workers to either stretch themselves further or to informally let something slide. It is better to estimate how much effort will be needed for work and to subtract that amount from the available time a worker has until he is fully engaged. This does not prevent stretch goals—time estimates can be a bit challenging. It does, however, prevent workers from second guessing what work is most important to the organization. By explicitly helping workers prioritize their activities, the most critical work is accomplished first. Also, by estimating how much time will be required for each project or process, each worker will be fully utilized and few will be overwhelmed. The maximum feasible amount of work will be selected considering the company's resources. People who are new to estimating work effort will learn over time how to estimate accurately. You might anticipate the early efforts may be overly optimistic on some people's part and overly cautious by other people. Part of the art of overseeing the resource issue is to develop a sense for both optimistic and overly cautious estimating and make adjustments.

### Governing Projects and Other Work

A typical dilemma for executives is to determine how to control important work without spending too much valuable executive time and without micromanaging. We choose to describe this as governing—more indirectly influencing work rather than extensive hands-on control. Part of portfolio management is establishing a system that will give executives insight into how work is progressing without intruding more than necessary. Many organizations already have monitoring, reporting, and governing systems in place. If you do and it works, use it.

If not, start with your most critical projects and ask what do you need to understand to make sure adequate progress (in terms of quality especially, but also in terms of cost and schedule) is being made. Two terms may help to visualize this: milestone and vital signs. In medieval England landowners would pay contractors to build roads. When the contractor said a mile was complete, the landowner would hire an assessor to both measure the length and to determine if the quality was good enough. Thus, the term milestone refers to both the quality and amount of work. On the critical projects in your company, ask what those milestones are that help you determine both quality and quantity. Note, the term is not yard stones—don't try to have reporting too often. An example milestone list with acceptance criteria is shown in Table 2.1.

*Table 2.1. Milestones in Project Management*

| Milestone | Acceptance criteria |
|---|---|
| Business plan approved | Budget approval<br>Process approval |
| Space procured | Meets space needs |
| Staffing recruited and trained | Staff identified, hired, and trained |
| Communication plan implemented | All user departments verify they understand |
| Shipping center launched | Fiscally acceptable<br>Compliant with regulation |

Vital signs are what a paramedic may check when arriving in an ambulance. While there are many medical checks that could be performed, the medic would likely check for pulse, breathing, and perhaps skin color to quickly assess the patient. More extensive tests can be done later by doctors and nurses. In the same way, what are the project's vital signs you want to check as an executive and what are the more detailed things your workers and managers can check?

## How Portfolio Management Is Accomplished

At an appropriate level all organizations can benefit from using a portfolio approach to select and manage work activities. Most commonly, the major selection, prioritization, and resourcing decisions are initially made once per year as part of strategic planning. They are often updated either periodically (such as quarterly or even monthly as part of regular meetings) or with changing conditions. The oversight role and new project identification ideally, are conducted continually as part of normal work. Ideally, everyone in the organization should be involved in identifying possible projects to help achieve organizational objectives and in carrying out some of the work. Managers should also propose the specific projects identified in their part of the organization along with planning and managing the projects. Executives should set the strategy, then select and prioritize the projects to achieve the strategy, and provide oversight of the work to ensure desired results.

### Objectives, Goals, Strategies, and Measures (OGSMs)

A frequently used strategic planning methodology, shown in Figure 2.2, will help illustrate how an organization's strategy can be implemented through a portfolio. The methodology is known by the acronym OGSM, which stands for objectives, goals, strategies, and measures.

An example of OGSM is shown in Figure 2.3 for a fictitious company.[5]

The natural use of having an agreed-to OGSM is to generate projects needed to accomplish the selected strategies and hitting the stated quantitative measures of success. Each of these projects needs to be owned not only by the project manager but also by an identified sponsor from the organization's leadership team. (See chapter 3 for a thorough discussion of the role of sponsors.)

Just because these OGSM projects are identified and developed does not mean that every such project will be selected to be staffed and funded. These projects will go through the same rigorous evaluation that all portfolio projects need to be subjected to.

Once an OGSM project has been selected, there is a process of OGSM reviews that needs to be employed. There is a quarterly review process for each strategy to see if the plans in place are sufficient to meet the defined success goals. The individual projects will have monthly

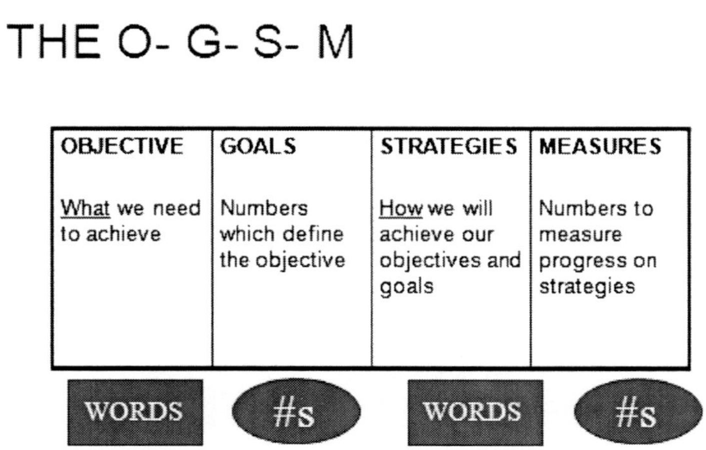

## THE O- G- S- M

| OBJECTIVE | GOALS | STRATEGIES | MEASURES |
|---|---|---|---|
| What we need to achieve | Numbers which define the objective | How we will achieve our objectives and goals | Numbers to measure progress on strategies |

WORDS   #s   WORDS   #s

Figure 2.2. The OGSM methodology.

| Objectives | Goals | Strategies | Measures | | Strategy owner |
|---|---|---|---|---|---|
| Be one of the top 2 widget servicing companies in the world, delivering superior quality repairs and thereby delivering superior returns to our shareholders | Double revenue every 10 years and double dividends every five years<br><br>Revenue / Dividends<br>2010  2,345 / 197<br>2011  2,533 / 227<br>2012  2,735 / 261 | 1.0 Build core electronics services business in line with new installations and increase profitablility to 22% by 2013 | Revenues / Profits<br>2010  1,800 / 360<br>2011  1,925 / 410<br>2012  2,080 / 460 | | Jane Smith |
| | | 2.0 Develop additional service business in the new 2nd generation hydraulic widgets market | | | Harry Jones |
| | | 2.1 Create plan and staff business for launch | 2.1 1st Quarter | | |
| | | 2.2 Evaluate acquisition targets and make decision on acquisition plans or JVs | 2.2 2nd Quarter | | |
| | | 3.0 Expand beyond North America to rest of world | | | Susan Black |
| | | 3.1 Create plan, including priority countries | 3.1 1st Quarter | | |
| | | 3.2 Begin operating in at least one country outside North America | 3.2 4th Quarter | | |
| | | 4.0 Increase Organizational Effectiveness | Revenue per employee<br>2011  200<br>2011  205<br>2012  210 | | Jim George |
| | | 4.1 Complete process redesign and reorganization | 4.1 2nd Quarter | | |
| | | 4.2 All employees complete training on working with an increasingly diverse company and client population | 4.2 3rd Quarter | | |
| | | 4.3 Double number of employees with official widget certification | 4.3 3rd Quarter | | |

*Figure 2.3. An example OGSM.*

reviews to assess if these projects are progressing well or need intervention by their sponsors.

### Scoring Models

A simple, yet comprehensive method leaders often use to select and prioritize projects involves a spreadsheet and is often called either a scoring model or a prioritization matrix. Scoring models are the one method that simultaneously considers maximizing the value of a portfolio and strategic alignment[6] as shown in Figure 2.4.

The concept behind scoring models is that more than one criterion is generally appropriate when selecting an optimal work portfolio. Scoring models facilitate:

- Consideration of both quantitative and qualitative factors,
- Sensitivity analysis by allowing executives to change criteria or weights,
- Addition or deletion of projects from consideration,
- Easy reprioritizing with changing conditions,

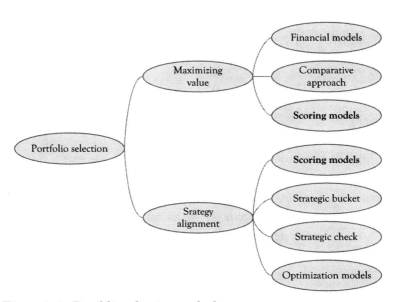

*Figure 2.4. Portfolio selection methods.*

- Active discussion and interpretation of each considered project, and
- Reporting, since project managers will be expected to report according to selection criteria.

Identifying Potential Projects

Executives will often consider both project success measures and risk limitation measures when determining selection criteria. An expanded view of project success measures was introduced in chapter 1. Some of these measures such as meeting specifications are very operational while others such as project team member loyalty to the company may be more strategic.

Careful development of selection criteria helps a company "do the right projects." Considering both project success measures and a desire to achieve those goals with an acceptable level of risk, useful project selection criteria might include:

- Alignment generally with the long-term organizational strategic direction,
- Alignment with one specific short- or medium-term organizational goal,
- Predicted return on investment,
- Probability of being successful,
- Access to necessary resources, and
- Image, social, ethical, or sustainability issues.

The process ideally starts with the organization's leadership deciding what criteria will be used to select projects and the relative weight or importance of each. An easy way to determine the importance of each is to use a 10-point scale and have the executives reach agreement on which one or two criteria are most important and assign a weight of 10 to that (or those) criteria. Then, the executive team would compare each other possible criterion and weight each in comparison to the most important. If one is almost as important, it might be weighted eight, if half as important, it might be weighted five. Generally any criterion that is weighted less than five is withheld as it probably will have little influence. It can be kept in reserve to help break ties if the team wishes. Generally the top three to five criteria are enough for a good analysis.

At this point, the executive team may communicate the criteria to everyone in the company so everyone can propose potential projects. Each proposed project should be accompanied by a very brief "elevator pitch." While the amount of detail will vary from one company to another, this generally refers to a short description of what the project entails (sometimes called the statement of work) and why it is important to the company (sometimes called the business case). The "why" is often described in comparison to the criteria by which the projects will be selected. If a large number of potential projects are raised to the leadership team (many dozens), either the team needs to ask the leaders of the various departments or divisions to screen the proposals in their areas to have a smaller number to consider or they need very short elevator pitches. At the point of project selection, the emphasis for a particular project from the executive's point of view needs to be how it will contribute to the overall goals of the company and a rough estimate of the resources it will need. Later, when the project is authorized via acceptance of a charter, the project manager and sponsor will need to also agree on the major deliverables that will be created by the project and how each will be judged. This will be the basis for executives to control the project. The project manager will plan in much more detail and will manage based upon that detail. A very simple elevator pitch example is below.

---

### Project Elevator Pitch

**Project Name: Creation of Biological Inventory Management System**

**Project Statement of Work** (What products or services will the project provide or improve?)

This project will create and test the accuracy of a biological inventory management system. The system will include a user-friendly input interface, but will not interface with any existing systems.

**Project Business Case** (Why is this project worth the investment?)

This system is primarily needed for accurate and timely reporting to regulatory agencies and will also improve employee productivity, satisfaction, and safety.

## Selecting and Prioritizing Identified Projects

To select the projects, the executives would use a spreadsheet like the one below. The spreadsheet illustrates five projects being evaluated on four selection criteria. The criteria the executives are using appear in columns across the top along with the weights ranging up to 10. Each potential project is listed down the left column. Then the executives rate each project on each criterion.

An accurate and easy way to do this is to compare projects on one criterion at a time and use a simple scale. A five-point scale is often used, with five meaning the project appears to be very strong on that criterion and one meaning the project appears to be very weak or noncontributing on that criterion. It is often quickest to provide the executives with a printed spreadsheet and let them have a few minutes to individually score the projects. By first determining the projects at both ends of the scale—those that very well support the criterion and those that have little or nothing to offer for that criterion, the executives often find it easier to rate the others in comparison.

Then a facilitator would generally ask for the scores of each project. A quick way to do this is to ask for the ones and fives first so the team can concentrate on the "gray area." When the executives share their scores, if there is a difference of one or two points on the five point scale, the average can be recorded with no added discussion. However, if there is a difference of three or four on the five-point scale, the executives who scored that project both highest and lowest are asked for their rationale. Often, one executive either knows or assumes something the others do not. Frequently the differences can be easily resolved. If not, mark that project as one with differing opinions to return to later if needed.

Once the scores for each project are recorded, each would be multiplied by the criterion weight. Then the team evaluates each potential project on each of the other criteria in turn. Finally, they summarize across the rows to obtain a total score for each potential project. The spreadsheet can then be sorted by total scores to show the order of preference for the projects. This order is the start, but not the total analysis. Generally the top scoring projects are clearly worth funding and the bottom few are not. The challenge is to sort through the projects in the middle that received very similar total scores. The executives need to use their judgment, any tiebreaker criteria, and any situation specific knowledge they possess to make these final decisions.

A few points can be understood by looking at the filled-in example in Figure 2.5. First, sometimes a project is a "must do" project. That means, a regulator will shut down the business or for some other overriding reason, there is no choice. The simple way to deal with "must do" projects is to rate them as a five on all criteria and they will automatically be selected first. The caution on "must do" projects is to make sure they really are since some people will try to slip their pet project in under the guise of "must do." Second, some projects may score very well on one criterion and very poorly on another. Third, there may be many ties, especially if quite a few projects are evaluated. Fourth, an executive team may need to think carefully about what a particular criterion means for a particular project. Remember the higher score means it fits that criterion very well. For example, consider risk on the remove asbestos project. Perhaps the risk of not doing the project is quite high—and therefore, this project scores well on the risk criterion. On the other hand, the project that deals with early research on a new cleaning method may be unlikely to find a technological breakthrough, and be rated poor on risk. Finally, projects of a particular type may generally score better than others. In this example, upgrade server and replace furnace scored high. These may be important, but for a company to continue to improve capability in the long run, upgrades and replacements may not be enough. In short, scoring models are extremely useful starting points, but executives need to exert judgment when using them.

| | New technology | Risk | ROI | Process improvement | |
|---|---|---|---|---|---|
| | 10 | 7 | 6 | 5 | Total |
| Upgrade server | 4 | 3 | 4 | 5 | |
| | 40 | 21 | 24 | 25 | 110 |
| Replace furnace | 3 | 4 | 4 | 5 | |
| | 30 | 28 | 24 | 25 | 107 |
| Research new cleaning method | 5 | 1 | 2 | 4 | |
| | 50 | 7 | 12 | 20 | 89 |
| Create new color | 5 | 2 | 1 | 1 | |
| | 50 | 14 | 6 | 5 | 75 |
| Remove asbestos | 1 | 5 | 2 | 2 | |
| | 10 | 35 | 12 | 10 | 67 |

*Figure 2.5. A sample project selection matrix.*

## Resourcing and Authorizing Selected and Prioritized Projects

Armed with the projects sorted in descending order according to total score, the executives can now begin to assign resources to the projects. The executives assigning resources would start with the highest priority project. This normally is the project that received the most points in the prioritizing or a "must do" project.

In some organizations resourcing is delegated, but in many organizations at least key individuals are assigned by the executive team. One reason for this is, generally there are not enough key individuals to staff all of the projects. When that happens, it is best to consider all of the projects as there may be a good reason to skip a project and start one with fewer total points first. Starting with the projects that receive the most points and working down ensures that the projects of the highest deemed importance are performed first. What often happens is the organization runs out of key resources (often an engineering manager or other technical leader first) before all desired projects can be started. In those cases, the executive team normally looks at the last couple of projects on the list that are tentatively resourced and the first couple of projects that are not and discuss which of those projects will be assigned resources first. In the example in Figure 2.6, the "create new color" project is tentatively resourced, while the "remove asbestos" project is not. The executive team

Project resource assignment template
Fiscal year quarter _____

|  | Paul | Tony | Percy | Schabaka | Ivan |
|---|---|---|---|---|---|
| Available hours for quarter | 120 | 480 | 180 | 120 | 120 |
| Total hours committed | 120 | 360 | 180 | 120 | 120 |
| Total hours exceeeding available | 0 | 120 | 0 | 0 | 0 |
| **Project list** | | | | | |
| Upgrade server | 60 | 360 | | | |
| Replace furnace | | | 60 | 120 | |
| Research new cleaning method | | | 60 | | 120 |
| Create new color | 60 | | 60 | | |
| Remove asbestos | | | | | |

*Figure 2.6. Assigning resources.*

would probably discuss whether they agree with that or if they want to make some adjustments. The projects with very high scores generally are quickly resourced and those with very low scores are generally deferred. The executives ideally spend time discussing the ones in the grey area in the middle.

## Governing Authorized Projects

Once projects are resourced, they would then go through a chartering process as discussed in chapter 3. Chartering includes deciding what on the project will be measured and when the measurements will be conducted. The milestones listed in a project charter are often great measurement points. Distinct points in the project life cycle can also be excellent measurement points. Remember to use the vital signs approach as it may be tempting to have the project manager report on many items. That takes time for both the project team to prepare for the progress reports and for the sponsor and/or executive team to review the progress. Possible items for reporting are shown in Figure 2.7.[7]

The executive team needs to keep several things in mind as they oversee the company's work portfolio. They must place interests of the company before department interests—they are representing the company as a whole. They need to ensure the company's strategy is reflected in the selected projects. They need to consider all risks as some project managers may be overly optimistic. They maintain a master list of all projects being performed. Finally, on the resource side, they may appoint sponsors and project managers. In some companies, the executive team may even appoint other project participants. In short, the executive team is ultimately responsible for all the work performed in the company.

| Project gate/BSC category | Customer | Internal project | Finance | Growth/innovation |
|---|---|---|---|---|
| Initial project selection | Statement of work | | Business case | Organisation's people and systems |
| End of initiating stage | • Scope overview<br>• Business case<br>• Stakeholder acceptance criteria | • High-level risks<br>• Commitment | • Milestone schedule<br>• Summary budget | • Team preassignment<br>• Previous lessons learned |
| End of planning stage | • Requirements documentation<br>• Scope baseline<br>• Work breakdown structure<br>• Communication of management plan | • Human resources plan<br>• Change management plan<br>• Risk management plan<br>• Risk register<br>• Quality management plan with metrics<br>• Procurement management plan<br>• Project management plan | • Schedule baseline with resources<br>• Cost performance baseline | • Team ground rules<br>• Improve management of project meetings<br>• Project kick-off |
| During executing | • Quality control measurements<br>• Stakeholder notification and feedback<br>• Project reports and records<br>• Validated deliverables | • Contract awards<br>• Performance information<br>• Change requests<br>• Risk register updates<br>• Procurement documentation | • Performance measures through earned value analysis<br>• Project termination decision | • Team performance assessments<br>• Process improvement<br>• Replanning<br>• Lessons learned application |
| End of executing stage | • Accepted deliverables<br>• Initial realization of promised benefits | • Complete project deliverables | • Project termination decision<br>• ROI | • Celebration<br>• Reward |
| End closing | • Ongoing support<br>• Customer feedback | • Final transition project deliverables<br>• Closed procurement | • Contract closure<br>• Final project accounting | • Capture lessons learned<br>• Reassign workers |
| During leveraging | • Full benefits realized | • Reuse | • Auditable result | • Reapplication of lessons |

*Figure 2.7. Possible reporting items for project progress reviews.*

# Duke Energy Case to Utilize a Work Portfolio

During Duke Energy's extensive annual Planning efforts, a rolling three-year capital project portfolio is developed to define the investment requirements of the electric Transmission and Distribution system. The budgeting and project selection process is used to ensure available capital is carefully scrutinized and applied to those projects providing the greatest strategic value in a timeframe minimizing risk in key areas. Maintaining the forecasted budget and completing projects as planned ensures the integrity of the electrical system and the financial strength of the business.

The project selection process is conducted year-round as Planners, Engineers, Project Managers, and financial experts balance multiple competing objectives into a rational, achievable, and ongoing capital spending plan. Annual spend for major capital projects may typically reach $500 million and represent over 1000 projects to be completed across the six-state service area. Under-budgeting means that projects potentially critical to the reliability of the electrical network may not be completed. Over-budgeting could result in investment dollars not yielding return and reducing earnings.

To enable this entire process to work continuously and effectively, the utility adopted a project portfolio optimization process to create, analyze, and refine the project portfolio to align with capital deployment and organizational strategies. This process involves executive management in assigning a weight to strategic value and risk scoring methodology used in evaluating all projects requiring capital. The method assigns a value and risk "score" based on each individual project's forecasted impact in five critical strategic impact areas—Financial, Reliability, Customer, Regulatory, and System Operations. A computer-based mathematical algorithm is used to optimize all possible spend portfolios to maximize value and minimize risk at specified budget levels. Within hours, the utility can analyze multiple optimized budget scenarios at various annual spend levels involving thousands of projects over multiple years.

The format of the project evaluation matrix is shown in the simplified example in Table 2.2. The optimization utilizes the following information to determine the "value/risk efficiency frontier" with regard to available capital.

- The forecast capital needs of the project in the budget year.
- The weighted strategic value of each project.
- The weighted strategic risk of deferring each project.

*Table 2.2. Simplified Value/Risk Project Portfolio Optimization Model*

| Project description | Planning year project cost ($Millions) | Project value — Strategy areas and weighting | | | | | Weighted value score | Project deferral risk — Strategy areas and weighting | | | | | Weighted risk score | Combined weighted risk score |
|---|---|---|---|---|---|---|---|---|---|---|---|---|---|---|
| | | Financial impact 40% | Reliability impact 20% | Customer impact 20% | Regulatory impact 10% | System performance 10% | | Financial impact 40% | Reliability impact 20% | Customer impact 20% | Regulatory impact 10% | System performance 10% | | |
| Midwest warehouse expansion | $5.50 | 7 | 7 | 7 | 2 | 4 | 6.20 | 7 | 7 | 7 | 9 | 4 | 6.90 | 13.10 |
| Enterprise IT upgrades | $10.00 | 4 | 8 | 3 | 8 | 8 | 5.40 | 9 | 8 | 3 | 8 | 8 | 7.40 | 12.80 |
| Equipment replacements | $16.40 | 8 | 1 | 3 | 5 | 5 | 5.00 | 5 | 4 | 3 | 5 | 5 | 4.40 | 9.40 |
| Southern region land purchases | $3.00 | 2 | 4 | 5 | 8 | 5 | 3.90 | 8 | 4 | 6 | 4 | 5 | 6.10 | 10.00 |
| Northern region equipment upgrades | $16.90 | 9 | 1 | 5 | 5 | 5 | 5.80 | 5 | 3 | 6 | 5 | 6 | 4.90 | 10.70 |
| Midwest customer interface system | $9.00 | 2 | 6 | 9 | 9 | 9 | 5.60 | 7 | 7 | 10 | 9 | 9 | 8.00 | 13.60 |
| Planning year budget limit | $25.00 | | | | | | | | | | | | | |
| Selected project spend forecast | $24.50 | | | | | | | | | | | | | |

### Lessons Learned

The major lessons learned in this case are:

1. The process starts with an annual review by executive management of the strategy categories to which value and risk assessments will be applied. These categories and their relative importance weightings can be adjusted to match the organization's current strategic emphasis. These categories and the relative weightings are published, communicated, and used as the standard throughout the organization.

   *Lesson Learned:* Management involvement in defining and weighting project selection strategy factors depicting the current business environment is essential for all subsequent analysis.

2. The scores of value and risk for each individual project are factored with the strategy category weightings. The data for all projects is then optimized to provide maximum value and minimum risk for the capital available. Computer applications allow instant scenario changes and "what if" options to be analyzed. The outcome provides management with consistent and well-understood decision-making information applied equally to all projects in all areas.

   *Lesson Learned:* Year-Round entry and management of project selection data allows capital spend strategy discussions to occur whenever needed with updated strategic priorities.

3. Projects are submitted for budget consideration in the capital portfolio from throughout the utility's six-state operating area. There is a diverse array of business and financial reasons for each project to be evaluated. The use of a single enterprise-wide tool allows all projects to be analyzed on an equal basis providing assurance that the organizational strategy is universally applied.

   *Lesson Learned:* Organizationally standardizing on project scoring criteria allows comparative discussions about project priorities across geographies and diverse business areas.

4. Postponing projects to conserve capital brings with it certain risks. The budget optimization process provides detailed risk analysis information on all deferred projects. Widespread communication of these risks and expert analysis of the consequences

*(Continued)*

(*Continued*)

and probability allow management to make calculated and carefully considered decisions. Importantly, management gains recognition of its own risk tolerance and risk threshold levels as a result.

*Lesson Learned:* Management teams cannot anticipate or approach the appropriate risk tolerance level of the organization without being presented with standardized value and risk information for each project.

5. The most significant result of the budget optimization process may well be the certainty to which implementation (the project execution phase) of the budget plan can be approached. The high levels of upfront management scrutiny leave little doubt about executive support for the plan going forward. This enables the planning horizon to be significantly expanded into future years and brings with it an enormous level of labor and material purchasing power in the market.

*Lesson Learned:* The project selection process allows the capital planning horizon to be significantly extended, with ensuing spend certainty providing supply chain and sourcing advantages.

6. Although the three-year budget plan is updated annually, there remain elements of uncertainty associated with implementation of a large project portfolio. These changes might be items such as significant shifts in public policy or regulations, fundamental changes to the business model, unexpected weather events, etc. These midstream shifts can be dealt with readily, if needed, by changing project scoring criteria, re-optimizing the project mix and re-evaluating the resulting information for options going forward.

*Lesson Learned:* Multiple scenarios and what-if simulations can be performed in anticipation of potential business changes to provide advanced planning opportunities.

*Lesson Learned:* Perhaps the greatest value of the project portfolio optimization process is that it provides a consistent and structured format for Management to engage in discussions regarding key strategic decisions with regard to project spending and the value and risk impact on organizational objectives.

Paul R. Kling PE, PMP
Director—Power Delivery Project Management & Controls
Duke Energy

# How Managing a Work Portfolio Helps Achieve Competing Objectives

### Executives Setting Strategy and Managers Implementing It

As part of project proposals, managers need to articulate how each potential project will help achieve the organization's strategic goals and executives who select and prioritize the projects need to explicitly rate each project on each criteria. Also, when both managers and executives understand reporting vital signs at milestones, enough information will be exchanged without micromanaging and without using undo time.

### Sustainable Organizational Capability and Achieving Current Business Results

All types of projects are considered and a mix of projects is selected to achieve each of those goals. It can be made abundantly clear that certain operational work needed to produce for current demand and possibly a very few critical projects will be automatically selected first, but after that, other operational work and all other project work will compete for the same resources.

### Project Goals and Operational Goals

Resources constrain both types of work and these resource constraints limit the number of projects that can be selected. When leaders carefully select, prioritize, resource, and govern all of the work of the organization as a portfolio, they have the ability to determine which projects and other work have goals that are most consistent with the overall goals of the organization.

### One Function's Goals and Another Function's Goals

All organizational projects need to go through the same selection and prioritization process competing with each other for resources. Also, many times when all potential work is considered, executives can see how two projects from different areas are related and encourage cooperation.

# Top 10 Portfolio Assessment Questions

1. How do you identify potential projects and how many of your work associates are actively involved in this identification?
2. How do you determine criteria for project selection?
3. What quantitative and qualitative criteria would you use for project selection?
4. What process do you use to select among potential projects?
5. How formally and consistently do you prioritize among selected projects?
6. How do you determine if you have enough resources—both financial and human—to perform the projects you select?
7. What are the project's vital signs you want to check as an executive and what are the more detailed things your workers and managers can check?
8. How do you work with your people to make sure they do not have way too much work on their plate?
9. How do you control and manage risk for selected projects? What vital signs will help you manage project risk?
10. Using the OGSM model, how will you assess if the strategies you have are sufficient to achieve your objectives measureable goals? What will you do if they are not sufficient?

# CHAPTER 3

# Sponsoring Successful Projects

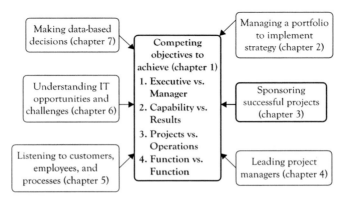

Often, an executive wants the results of a project because either they will be used in her part of the organization or they will be delivered to an important client. This executive will often serve as the project sponsor by providing both the resources and guidance that will enable a project manager to successfully plan and implement the necessary work. This chapter deals with the behaviors a busy executive sponsor can use to leverage his time while a project manager and team develop and deliver project results. The purpose of this chapter is to help you:

- Determine the duties, motivations, and challenges of the sponsor's role and
- Determine the high value activities you can engage in as a sponsor at each stage in the project life cycle.

## TriHealth Case to Determine Sponsor Responsibilities

TriHealth is a company that manages several large hospitals and related health care facilities. The role of project/initiative leaders or champions has not been well understood within TriHealth. Executives have varying experiences and approaches to this role, which can lead to confusion, suboptimization, and ineffective leadership and coordination of critical projects and initiatives the organization needs to accomplish. Management and staff who work under these leaders on project or initiative teams can experience varying approaches, expectations, and success levels, which can lead to frustration and poor outcomes.

TriHealth, its management teams, and staff would benefit from a more consistent and well-understood set of project leadership roles.

**The key question TriHealth leaders faced** is how can they leverage the precious time of their executives in effort to increase the rate of success of their projects? This is the classic sponsorship question and the subject of this chapter.

## Project Sponsors

One way to understand the role of a sponsor is to envision the sponsor and project manager as a team. The sponsor is generally a high-ranking executive or manager with significant organizational knowledge and influence. The project manager is generally a lower level manager or even individual contributor who is at the center of most project communications and activities, but does not often enjoy significant organizational position power. Generally speaking the sponsor has more power, but less time to devote to the project. The project manager, by contrast, devotes a proportionately greater amount of time to the project but wields considerably less power.

The most essential lesson concerning the partnership of sponsor and project manager is that what they each bring to the project is complementary but distinct. One person should not attempt to do both jobs no matter how short the organization may be on resources! When a sponsor is also the direct supervisor of the project manager, she performs the project executive role as well. The next chapter describes the project executive role. Frequently, however, these are two different executives each of whom needs to work effectively with the project manager and with each other.

### Sponsor Standard Definitions

A classic, yet limited definition of the sponsor is "the person or group that provides the financial resources, in cash or in kind, for the project."[1] Yet this same global source, the *PMBOK® Guide,* also lists several responsibilities of the sponsor:

- Champion the project,
- Serve as a spokesperson to higher management,
- Gather support and promote benefits for the project,
- Lead the project through the selection process,
- Play a significant role in developing the initial charter and scope,
- Serve as an escalation for issues beyond the project manager's control,
- Authorize changes,
- Conduct phase-end reviews, and
- Make go/no-go decisions.[2]

The standard United Kingdom (UK) source, the Office of Government Commerce (OGC) seeks to operationalize the sponsor's role from the UK project management standard (PRINCE2) by listing many project sponsor responsibilities, purpose of the sponsor role, and useful skills and attributes for a sponsor to possess. In addition to the responsibilities listed above, the OGC emphasizes the sponsor's role in representing clients and end-users, dealing with risks and budgets, and both partnering with and managing the project manager.[3]

### Sponsor Definitions from Research

The sponsor has also been described as "a senior business executive with executive experience… who serves as a mentor, catalyst, motivator, barrier buster, boundary manager and … change leader. Being a project sponsor is to be involved from project initiation to the end."[4] This suggests that not only does a sponsor have many responsibilities, but that they last over the life of a project and some of them may vary from one point in the project life to another.

Researchers have been investigating which of the many suggested sponsor behaviors lead most directly to project success. These behaviors have been grouped into internal to the company versus external activities[5] or dimensions such as leadership, resource alignment, scope management, etc.[6]

Finally, some researchers have combined the ideas of looking at which sponsor behaviors at each point in the project life cycle contribute to project success.[7–10] Busy executives are able to focus their efforts when they understand the few critical sponsor behaviors that help projects succeed and the timing of each.

### Applied Sponsor Definition for this Book

The sponsor is the executive who provides resources for a project. The sponsor, in combination with the project manager and project executive, is responsible for delivering project results. The sponsor, though a busy executive, has a few specific project responsibilities starting with project selection and continuing through realization of project benefits.

## Sponsor Responsibilities by Project Stage

To fully understand these responsibilities and the timing of each, we now review important sponsor behaviors both overall and at each stage in the project life cycle as depicted in Table 3.1.

### Sponsor Overarching Responsibilities

First and foremost, a sponsor needs to provide the necessary resources to a project and is responsible for delivering results. In both of these responsibilities the sponsor is the link between the parent organization and the project. Resources can include money, space, equipment, and personnel with adequate training and experience. Delivering results can include making sure the project manager and team have the means in place to monitor and control the project; to stay personally informed regarding the project progress; and to partner with the project manager and project executive in determining how to overcome problems. The project manager is also responsible for delivering results, but the sponsor cannot

*Table 3.1. Sponsor Responsibilities by Project Stage*

| Stage | Sponsor responsibilities | Stage ending gate |
|---|---|---|
| Overarching | Provide resources, deliver results | |
| Selecting | Identify, select, prioritize projects | Project selected |
| Initiating | Mentor PM, charter project | Charter ratified |
| Planning | Meet stakeholder, ensure planning | Plan approved |
| Executing | Nurture stakeholders, ensure communications, ensure quality | Deliverables accepted |
| Closing | Ensure satisfaction, closure, and knowledge management | Project closed |
| Leveraging benefits | Ensure benefits achieved and capability increased | Benefits realized |

wash his hands and demand the project manager perform unilaterally. Some companies are serious enough about the sponsor role that a (usually small) percentage of executive compensation is tied to how well the projects sponsored by each executive perform.

The sponsor is the link between senior management and the project team. The sponsor is also the link between the customer and the project team. Serving as these links, the sponsor provides resources and delivers results as overarching duties throughout the project life. This may include help behind the scenes obtaining resources and removing road blocks as well as visible participation in meetings where the sponsor announces decisions regarding resources and listens to progress reports as a means of emphasizing the need to deliver planned results. We will now discuss the two or three specific types of behaviors sponsors can use at each project stage to help ensure project success.

## Sponsor Selecting Stage Responsibilities

Selecting projects starts whenever any person has the germ of an idea and ends when projects are initially selected for inclusion in the organization's work portfolio. Selecting projects includes identifying, selecting, and prioritizing a portfolio of projects that will, hopefully, best help the company meet its goals. Both the rationale and mechanics of performing these three activities are covered in chapter 2. The sponsor, who is often a member of a leadership team, both works personally to perform some of these duties and helps to create an atmosphere and expectation for others. Everyone who works for a company should be on the lookout for potential projects. A sponsor, as an executive, can encourage this behavior. The sponsor can also personally identify potential projects. If the sponsor is part of the leadership team, she generally participates in selecting and prioritizing projects.

### Sponsor Initiating Stage Responsibilities

Initiating projects begins when projects are selected for inclusion in the organization's work portfolio and ends when a project is officially launched by a charter that is signed by the sponsor, project manager, and core team members. The first essential sponsor behavior when initiating a project is to select and mentor the project manager. The other essential behavior is to charter the project.

### Select and Mentor Project Manager

Chapter 4 describes how an executive can directly supervise a project manager. In this section, we just cover how a sponsor can select and mentor a project manager. In many cases, the project manager is not a direct report to the sponsor—so the traditional supervisor–employee relationship may not exist.

Remember, the sponsor is often a member of an executive steering team. In many organizations, the executive team will jointly decide who should manage each project. The sponsor, as a member of that team, has a say. Sometimes a project executive will offer one of her direct reports as the project manager. Often, the other executives will defer to the sponsor's judgment just as they would like to have other executives defer to them on their projects. In many smaller organizations, the choice of project manager may be obvious as there may only be one available person who has the experience necessary. In larger organizations, many thoughts might come into play.

- How critical and how complex is the project?
- Is this project a good assignment to help someone gain experience?
- Is the sponsor well-seasoned and capable of mentoring a rooky project manager?
- Will there be proven individuals who can be assigned to the project who can help mentor an inexperienced project manager?
- What specific project demands suggest a particular person is assigned as project manager?
- Is there an individual with untapped talent if the sponsor looks far enough?

Some project managers are selected based upon demonstrated technical success. Those people might or might not become effective project managers, but the sponsor can greatly increase the probability of success by helping them deal effectively with the broad range of stakeholders most projects have. The sponsor can role-model some of these skills and can create situations where the project manager is the focal point of the project and the sponsor is in a supporting role.

The sponsor also needs to continually reinforce how the project fits in the big picture of organizational goals. This will first be spelled out tersely in the charter. The sponsor can continue to reinforce this connection in many different informal ways. This will help most project managers as they, in turn, need to communicate project goals and needs with many other people.

The sponsor also needs to define project manager performance expectations. Part of this is accomplished through goals identified in the charter and then detailed more specifically later in project planning documents. Part of it, however, should be understood between the sponsor and the project manager. An effective sponsor/project manager partnership generally requires a great deal of informal dialog—especially early in the project. As the project manager proves more and more worthy of sponsor trust, the conversations can be less often and less detailed.

Charter Project

One of the most important project management documents is the charter. The charter is a high-level project preplanning document. The sponsor makes chartering easier if she starts the process by providing him understanding very briefly of what the project might deliver and why the project is important to the organization. If she has any other firm convictions (such as an approach to use or something to include), it is also helpful to share that with the project manager and team. Sponsors can effectively provide this information either in one page or less of suggestions and/or by attending the first part of a chartering meeting to speak with the project manager and team.

Charters are the gate between the initiating stage where the project becomes official and the planning stage in which detailed plans are developed. In most organizations, charters have little detail and are developed quickly. The purposes of a charter are:

- Authorization for a project manager to proceed with at least detailed project planning and perhaps with performing the project itself,
- Developing a common understanding at a high level of the project,
- Committing the sponsor, project manager, and core team to the project, and
- Quickly screening out projects that appear less practical when chartered than they did when selected.

While many organizations have developed customized charters, a basic charter may be envisioned as including the three Ws, Rs, and Cs as in Table 3.2.

**Table 3.2. The Three Ws, Rs, and Cs of Project Charters**

| 3 Ws | 3 Rs | 3 Cs |
|------|------|------|
| What | Risks | Communication needs |
| Why | Resources | Collection of knowledge |
| When | Routines | Commitment |

The first two elements are sometimes called the elevator pitch. These are what a person communicates to another on a short elevator ride when time is very limited. The most essential information about a project is what the project is trying to accomplish and why it is important. Each of these statements is typically about two to five sentences in length. What (sometimes called the scope overview) can be described in project deliverables or results whether tangible or not. The best why statements (sometimes called the business case) may include four thoughts:

1. The strategic alignment between the project and a goal of the parent organization.
2. The return on the investment of time, money, and other resources to complete the project.
3. An emotional hook so people stay engaged in the project even when things are difficult.
4. Any ethical reasons why the project should be undertaken.

This is often followed closely by describing how long it will take in the form of a milestone schedule. An essential component of the milestone schedule is a definition of how quality will be judged at each intermediate milestone. This emphasizes quality of the emerging work and not just schedule.

The charter continues with risks—primarily what can go wrong (threats) and how the company can capitalize upon the project (opportunities). Sometimes people will also discuss assumptions—unproven beliefs and/or constraints—what limits the project choices here. Resources in the form of money, people, and equipment or space often limit the project. The third R, routines, is how the project team will meet, make decisions, accomplish work, and treat each other with respect.

The charter also includes the three Cs. Communication needs are determined by listing and prioritizing project stakeholders along with what each stakeholder wants from the project. Learning organizations always strive to improve their capability by collecting knowledge of what worked well to repeat in future projects and what would work better if changed. Finally, when sponsors, project managers, and core team members sign a charter, they commit to the project.

The project manager and core team generally write the rough draft, the project manager (often with the project team) presents the charter to the sponsor (and maybe other executives), and then the project manager and sponsor negotiate the final charter. In some organizations, after the sponsor and project manager reach agreement, they present the charter together to the leadership team for approval. The sponsor typically signs the charter representing the leadership team.

When a project manager leads him team in developing the "what" and "why" statements, it is helpful to first brainstorm what they know or think about the project and to use key words and phrases from those discussions to compose statements about what the project will deliver and why it is important. The "when" section is both a milestone schedule and the corresponding quality requirements for completing the deliverable associated with each milestone. The quality requirements include both the acceptance criteria and the person who will make the acceptance determination. The first item on the milestone schedule is the current situation. The last item on the milestone schedule is the successful conclusion of the project or possibly even the ultimate goal if the project in question is planned just to get partway toward a more ambitious goal. The entire schedule shows how to close the gap between the current situation and expected future results.

On some projects, the milestones can be described rather easily. On others, the results of early work are needed to plan late work. The agile approach that is gaining popularity in project management places emphasis on clearly describing the first milestone(s) and letting the later milestones emerge. Sometimes, early milestones include either identifying optional approaches to the project and/or gathering more data so better decisions can be made. Sometimes, one of the later milestones is how to capitalize on the results of the project beyond the original project goals.

The "Three Rs" are risk, resources, and routines. At a minimum, the team should identify potential negative risks (threats) by brainstorming. Then, they use qualitative risk analysis to decide which risks are big enough that response plans need to be instituted to either reduce the probability of occurrence and/or impact on the project. Finally, the team agrees which of them is personally responsible for monitoring each of those big risks and implementing the response plans if needed. The resources needed for the project may be money, people, equipment, materials, space, etc. The team creates ball-park estimates of these needs. Finally, especially for teams that have not worked together, it is often helpful to describe the routines the team will use to operate effectively.

The "Three Cs" are communication needs, collection of knowledge, and commitment. The communication needs consist of identifying all of the stakeholders—those people and groups who are interested in the project process or results. The team brainstorms an exhaustive list of stakeholders, prioritizes them into primary and other, and then identifies what interests each have in the project. This stakeholder list will serve as the starting point in communications planning. Collection of knowledge is what worked well on previous projects to be repeated and what worked poorly on previous projects to be avoided. By consciously and explicitly discussing these lesson learned, project teams become better and better over time. Finally, signature blocks are created for the sponsor, project manager, and team. By signing the charter, each commits to the concept of the project. There are few details yet—so it is not like a legal contract. It is, however, like a moral contract with each party agreeing to do their best to live up to the spirit of the project. It is also like a moral contract in that it can be changed as long as both parties agree and there is some consideration for each. That means, if a business need forces an earlier than planned project finish or additional scope, the sponsor can ask the team to change in response to that business need. However, the sponsor will then help them figure out how to reprioritize other work, obtain other resources, or otherwise help them accomplish the new demands. A charter example follows.

**Project Charter: "Streamline New Hire On-Boarding Process in Research Division" Date: July 30, 2012.**

# What (Scope Overview)

This project will develop a streamlined and consistent system for orienting new hires and integrating them into a cohesive team structure. We will develop an on-boarding process, orientation manuals, and operating procedures.

# Why (Business Case)

A survey of managers indicates the belief that new employees in our research division are not fully productive until after three months of employment. We believe with a systematic on-boarding process employees can be fully productive after two months. This should return $4000 in more rapid productivity per new employee while reducing their frustration and increasing their job satisfaction.

## When (Milestone Schedule with Acceptance Criteria)

*Table 3.3. Milestone Schedule with Acceptance Criteria*

| Milestone | Completion date | Person judging | Acceptance criteria |
|---|---|---|---|
| **Current State:** Generic orientation | | | |
| Initial needs assessment | Aug 31, 2012 | HR director | All needs captured |
| Create specific orientation materials | Sep 28, 2012 | HR manager | Checklist complete |
| Create procedures for each hiring rank | Oct 31, 2012 | Research manager | Job duties complete |
| Train existing employees | Nov 30, 2012 | Education director | Post training test |
| All new hires on-boarded | Jan 7, 2013 | HR director | All new hires use |
| **Future State:** On-boarding system effective | Feb 28, 2013 | Research director (Sponsor) | 75% of new hires fully effective in 2 months |

## Risks

*Table 3.4. Project Risks*

| Major project risks | Risk owner | Contingency plans |
|---|---|---|
| 1. Unable to identify all needs | Tony D. (Project manager) | • Standardize criteria<br>• Establish timeline with directors |
| 2. Inadequate executive support | Madeline G. (Sponsor) | • Strongly advocate project value with directors at start<br>• Cancel project if needed |
| 3. Employee resistance | Jordan H. (Project team member) | • Demonstrate value of new member early effectiveness |

# Resources

- **Funding:** This project requires no cash funding except for training supplies of about $400.
- **People:** We estimate 300 hours of employee/manager time (fully loaded = $10,500), plus 30 hours of executive time (fully loaded = $2700).
- **Other:** This project requires time in existing conference training rooms (no cost).
- **Total:** $13,600.

# Routines (Team Operating Principles)

- All team members will have clearly defined roles and responsibilities.
- Each meeting will end with clear action items and due dates for each team member.
- The project team will determine in advance who will make each decision and by what means.
- The project team will meet weekly for 1 hour using advance agendas and recording minutes.

# Communication Needs (Stakeholders)

*Table 3.5. Communication Needs by Stakeholder*

| Stakeholders | Interest in project |
|---|---|
| Primary: Research managers, executive leadership team new employees | Timely progress on project Effectiveness of new process Clear understanding of expectations |
| Others: Existing employees HR and education directors and managers | Impact on their work Effectiveness of new process Specific training needs, Effectiveness of new process |

# Collection of Knowledge (Lessons Learned)

- The project team will devote time to building continual key stakeholder support.
- The project manager will speak candidly and informally to sponsor in addition to formal reports.

- The project team will be open to constructive criticism and other inputs from stakeholders.
- The project team will invite specific directors to key project meetings.

# Commitment

*Table 3.6. Commitment*

| Sponsor | Department/organization | Signature |
|---|---|---|
| Madeline G. | Research director | |
| **Project manager** | **Department/organization** | **Signature** |
| Tony D. | Education | |
| **Core team members** | **Department/organization** | **Signature** |
| Jordan H. | HR | |
| Lifang W. | Research | |
| Rashmi A. | Research | |

### Sponsor Planning Stage Responsibilities

The planning stage begins with a signed charter that signifies high-level agreement by the sponsor, project manager, and core team and ends with acceptance of the detailed project plans by all stakeholders. Much of the detail work in this stage is performed by the project manager, core team, subject matter experts, and other project stakeholders. The sponsor has two specific responsibilities during this stage. First is to look outward, understand who all of the stakeholders are, and to establish effective communication channels and working relationships with them. The other responsibility is to look inward to ensure the project is planned in the detail required.

### Establish Stakeholder Relations

Stakeholders were identified in the project charter, but as more detailed planning takes place, it is common to both uncover more stakeholders and more detailed understanding of their wants and needs. Stakeholders can be for or against the project. Sponsors want to reduce the influence of those opposed and capitalize upon the enthusiasm of those who are for a project. Stakeholders can have an interest in the project process (they may be inconvenienced or they may need to provide resources) or in the project deliverables (their work may be changed by the project results). Just as the business case includes both logical and emotional reasons for undertaking the project, stakeholders have both logical and emotional thoughts that need to be understood. Some stakeholders are critical to the project in that they can shut it down if displeased while others may be mere gadflies who make noise few consider.

Sponsors are responsible to ensure that all of the work identifying, understanding, and prioritizing stakeholders is accomplished and in as transparent a fashion as practical. The sponsor creates the environment in which effective communication can occur between the project team and the stakeholders so stakeholder input can be incorporated into project plans. The sponsor will personally communicate with more influential stakeholders and ensure that the project manager and team communicate effectively with the other stakeholders. Sponsors frequently find it useful to develop personal relationships with peers in the client and major supplier organizations.

## Ensure Planning

The other sponsor responsibility during the planning stage is to ensure that all necessary planning is performed. The sponsor will not personally do much of this—but needs to understand the depth of planning that makes sense for the project. A sponsor should have the team spend $100 in planning effort to save $1000 in project cost, but not the other way around. Both high-level and detailed project planning techniques exist for each of the following:

- Scope (requirements matrix, scope statement, work breakdown structure),
- Communications (stakeholder matrix, communication matrix, meeting management tools),
- Change (issues log, change request form),
- Schedule (network diagram, bar chart),
- People (responsibility matrix, individual and team assessment, resource loaded schedule),
- Cost (budget, supporting detail),

- Risk (risk identification, risk analysis, risk response plan),
- Quality (quality policy, quality baseline, quality assurance, quality control), and
- Reporting (project kick-off, progress report, earned value analysis).

### Sponsor Executing Stage Responsibilities

The executing stage begins when all stakeholders approve the detailed project plan and ends when the primary project customer formally accepts the main project deliverables. In reality, on many projects, the line between creating the plan and satisfying requirements is not so clean. Sometimes substantial work begins before the full plan is approved. Sometimes results of early work need to be understood before later work can be planned in detail. Sometime a decision is made to use rolling wave planning—that is, to plan a first little wave of work and complete that portion while planning the next wave. The extreme case of this, called agile project management, is becoming more popular especially with software development projects. At any rate, in this section, we focus on the sponsor responsibilities that occur when the project team is satisfying the agreed upon requirements. The three necessary sponsor behaviors at this time are to build upon the stakeholder relationships that were started during planning (or before), ensure effective communications occur, and ensure the quality of the project processes and results.

### Nurture Stakeholder Relations

One role of the sponsor is to champion the project. This includes reminding both the project team and many stakeholders why the project is needed. Sponsors personally focus on key stakeholders through individual communication, relationship building, and ensuring expectations are met. Sponsors deal with internal stakeholders by managing organizational politics, formally and informally updating the executive team on project progress, and authorizing execution of project activities. Sponsors also remember who the project deliverables are being created to serve. They ensure customers and users of the project deliverables remain involved as the project progresses and are updated on progress.

Ensure Effective Communications

Communications need to occur with the project team and manager and with other stakeholders. One of the most effective things a sponsor can do to aid communications is to visibly empower the project manager. A project manager with little power is like a weak coordinator who people only pay attention to when they want something. Sponsors can work with the project manager behind the scenes to develop communications strategies for specific people and situations. In public, showing confidence in the project manager and making it clear that the project manager speaks for the sponsor encourages many people to deal directly with the project manager. This saves precious time both for the sponsor and for the project schedule. Nevertheless, there are situations when a team member would like to give the sponsor direct feedback and this needs to be encouraged. Effective sponsors actively listen to team members both individually and as a team. Sponsors sometime need to re-focus teams when a project has drifted.

Sponsors also communicate with other stakeholders. One way is by supporting the project vision, helping people to progressively understand better what the project entails and why it is critical to both them as individual stakeholders and to the organization more broadly. Just as sponsors encourage input and actively listen to the project team, they do so with all stakeholders, both individually and in groups. There is a delicate balancing act here. On the one hand, the project manager needs to be the primary focal point of communication. On the other hand, when people know you are available to them, few will abuse the privilege and some of the sensitive issues that are brought to your attention will prevent problems.[11]

One major purpose of effective communications is to ensure progress. Several sponsor behaviors that help to ensure progress are:

- Resolve conflicts when escalated.
- Remove obstacles to project progress.
- Defend the project's priority.
- Communicate issues effectively with executives.[12]

## Lead for Quality

Sponsors can provide leadership for quality in four areas: ethics, decision-making, risk management, and quality control. Ethics leadership includes continually role-modeling and reminding people of the ethical standards that need to be used and then ensuring that they are, in fact, used. Sponsors also strive to ensure all disputes are resolved fairly, not showing favoritism or bias. Since many people work hard on most projects, it often seems fair to celebrate small wins. This can be coffee and donuts for a very small victory or something more substantial. People see justice in small rewards, not just for going through the motions, but also for delivering results.

Sponsors make some decisions and create the environment in which other decisions are made. Decisions often have a major impact on quality. Sponsors need to understand what resistance exists to particular decisions. Much of this understanding comes from the project manager, but sponsors need to keep their own channels of communication open to be aware of resistance. Whether the sponsor or project manager makes the decision, sponsors need to insist that consistent criteria and adequate information are used in the decision-making process. Most projects have schedule pressure, so decisions often need to be made with less than full information. Sponsors work with project managers to determine when enough information is available to make the decision.

Sponsors also need to insist that a change management system is used. On most projects, many potential changes need to be considered. An effective change management system requires that each potential change be proposed with any impact described. Then a decision-maker approves or does not approve the change. Any impact resulting from approved changes needs to be included in the current project plan and any unapproved change should not be slipped in by someone who did not take no for an answer. One trick with effective change control is to make the process as simple as possible. This can be accomplished by having a very simple change request form as shown in Figure 3.1 and making the approval decision transparent. Wise sponsors who have empowered their project managers let those project managers make most of the decisions with only controversial and major decisions being bumped up to the sponsor.

```
┌─────────────────────────────────────────────────────────────┐
│                      Change request form                     │
│  Date requested:                                             │
│  Description of change:                                      │
│                                                              │
│  Why needed:                                                 │
│                                                              │
│  Impact on schedule:                                         │
│  Impact on budget:                                           │
│  Impact on quality:                                          │
│  Other impacts:                                              │
│                                                              │
│  Approved by:                                                │
│  Project manager     Date    or    Sponsor        Date       │
│  _____              _____        │
└─────────────────────────────────────────────────────────────┘
```

*Figure 3.1. Sample change request form.*

Another aspect of quality leadership is how risks are managed. Risk identification, assessment, and resolution planning started at a high level during the initiating stage and became more detailed during the planning stage. This needs to continue during the executing stage as new risks will appear with changing circumstances. Also, monitoring the environment for the occurrence of risk events needs to be ongoing. Sponsors do not need to do much of this personally, but they need to make sure it happens. One good way is to have a member of the project core team assigned as the owner of each major risk. The risk owner should understand the triggers (or predictors) of the risk event. For example, a weather report predicting storms tomorrow is a likely trigger that it will rain. As the sponsor, it makes sense to ask for updates on major risks at progress meetings. The updates can include the triggers, but also the avoidance and mitigation strategies the project team plans to use.

Traditional quality control is also part of quality leadership. Sponsors do not need to be too involved in details—mostly just ensure these activities are completed. One specific action sponsors should insist on is root cause analysis. Demand to know, with data, why some problem happened and how the process is being changed so it will not happen again. This is not blaming individuals—it is improving the system. The other specific action sponsors require here is when a problem occurs, timely corrective action should follow. It is not enough to acknowledge a mistake—it is also important to rectify it quickly.

The sponsor's final part of quality leadership is to secure customer approval of the project deliverables. This final approval generally requires a demonstration to convince the key stakeholders that the project deliverables meet their needs. This also applies to internal projects with a client who works for the same company you do. If the project was creating a decision-support system, the client probably wants to run some of their data through it to make sure the outputs seem reasonable. If the project was creating a house, the client probably wants a walk-through with the construction supervisor to make sure everything looks good and works. On many projects, the client wants use of the deliverables before they are complete. When this happens, the client and project manager jointly develop and agree upon a "punch list" of items that still need to be finished. If the list is small, the client may accept the deliverables subject to the project team finishing the listed items during the closing stage. If the list is long or has important items on it, the client will probably not accept the deliverables yet and the project will remain in the executing stage.

### Sponsor Closing Stage Responsibilities

The project closing stage begins when the client formally accepts the major project deliverables—with or without a punch list of minor items remaining to be completed. This stage ends when all of the project objectives are met; stakeholders are satisfied with the project results; and resources are successfully transitioned. Alternatively, if the project was unsuccessful, it is terminated. In either event, part of the ending point is capturing knowledge for sharing with future projects.

Ensure Successful Transition

Successfully transitioning project results begins with ensuring they meet the needs of key stakeholders. While this was started at the transition into this stage when the client formally accepted the deliverables, it generally needs more attention as there was probably a "punch list" to be completed. Also, with many stakeholders on typical projects, it is still likely some are not happy. Understanding their needs and frustrations can help make a smoother transition. Not understanding their frustrations can lead to lack of user commitment and unsuccessful termination as described next. Successful sponsors have their project managers and teams document that all project objectives were accomplished perhaps with a checklist that is then archived. Then the project team develops a transition plan to help the customers successfully use the project results. This plan may include documentation, instruction, and mentoring.

The sponsor also wants to be sure project resources are successfully transitioned. Some of this is administrative with budgets and physical items being accounted for. A big part of it is taking care of the project manager and team. Evaluations need to be conducted with sponsor-generated input supplied for people's performance reports. Appropriate reassignments, promotions, bonuses, and celebrations may be in order. Smart sponsors understand that if they take care of their project managers and team members, it will be much easier to recruit and lead on future projects.

## Determine Unsuccessful Termination

A troubled project should be cancelled as soon as it is obvious it cannot deliver the needed benefits. Also, a project that is creating deliverables that are no longer needed or are no longer a top priority should be terminated as soon as this determination is made. This cancellation could happen during an earlier stage when knowledge gained during chartering or planning shows the project is impractical. It could occur during the executing stage when problems are occurring. Regardless of when it starts to become apparent that the project cannot succeed or is no longer needed, the sponsor should be one of the first people to question its viability. While the sponsor appropriately champions the project while it has a chance, once the sponsor determines it has no chance, it is time to act as an executive of the company and decide not to throw good money after bad.

If the project is terminated because the company's priorities have changed, the sponsor needs to ensure that the project manager and everyone working on the project are protected. It is both unethical and impractical to punish people for things beyond their control. However, if the project is cancelled because of failure to do proper work, there may be appropriate repercussions and the sponsor needs to be at the center of those decisions.

Ensure Knowledge Management

Effective companies are learning organizations. Sponsors realize that they need to capture lessons from work experiences and use those lessons to improve future phases of the existing project and future projects. "Learning is acquiring new or modifying existing knowledge, behaviors, skills, and values."[13] Projects provide wonderful opportunities to improve, as there is often a combination of routine and unique work performed at different stages. Lessons on a large project are often captured at the end of each life cycle stage or at the accomplishment of key milestones. Lessons on short, small projects may be captured just at the end. Lessons can be captured from both the project team and from other stakeholders. At any rate, sponsors need to insist that lessons are captured, categorized, stored, shared, and then used appropriately on future projects.

While there are many ways to capture lessons learned, one very simple technique often used is the plus delta method. A plus delta can be completed in a few minutes with one person facilitating. Using a work surface such as flip chart or white board, the person draws a large cross and places a plus sign (for good) above one side and a triangle (symbol of delta or change) above the other side as shown in Figure 3.2. Then the facilitator asks the team what worked well on the project that team members feel should be repeated on future projects. Likewise, he asks what worked poorly and should be improved on future projects. Responding to the pluses is easy—just smile and say thank you. The key to effectively capturing lessons learned is how one responds to the improvement suggestions. No sign of irritation should be displayed or there may not be many useful suggestions. The facilitator could paraphrase the suggestion to ensure understanding and then respond in one of several ways:

1. The most direct is to offer a possible method of making the improvement.
2. A second is to acknowledge the suggestion as useful, but ask the project team for guidance on how to implement it.
3. A third is to ask if everyone else agrees with the suggestion as it may be only one person's opinion.
4. A fourth possible response is to disagree, with a reason for the disagreement.

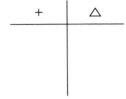

*Figure 3.2. Plus delta chart.*

Once lessons learned are captured, they should be categorized. Companies find that having a few categories is better than none or many. Examples of potential categories include: scope, schedule, cost, quality, stakeholder management, team management, communications, vendors, leadership, and operations.

After lessons are categorized, they need to be stored and distributed. Companies may use shared drives, wikis, databases, or other means. The key is to make this simple to both input lessons into and acquire lessons from whatever system you choose to use.

Perhaps the most essential sponsor responsibility with lessons learned is to insist they are used to change behavior. One easy way for sponsors to do this is to never sign a charter for a new project nor authorize the next phase of an existing project until the project manager and team describe at least one or two new lessons they have discovered in the lessons learned repository and discussed how they will improve based upon those lessons.

### Sponsor Leveraging Benefits Stage Responsibilities

The realizing benefits stage occurs weeks or months after the project is complete. The idea is to assess how well the end users of the project deliverables are able to use them. Were the benefits that were promised during project selection delivered? Has the client capability improved because of the project deliverables and has the company capability improved because of utilizing lessons learned from the project process? Have the project results been used in additional ways not originally predicted? Have any methods developed on the project been used in other settings?

## Ensure Benefits are Achieved

The primary reason projects are undertaken is that some users need deliverables they can use in performing their work. A sponsor should insist that an evaluation take place after the users have been conducting business with the project results for a period of time. The exact questions may be context-specific, but essentially the users should answer questions such as:

- Were the original proposed benefits achieved?
- Are the project deliverables worth the time and effort of development?
- Has market share or sales increased because of the project deliverables?
- Does the company have viable new products as a result of the project?
- Are the users able to use the project deliverables to satisfy their own customers?
- Are the users "selling" the project results to other stakeholders?

## Ensure Capability Is Increased

Capability improvements can be assessed for both the customer and the company performing the project. It can be measured both at the organizational level and at the project team member level. Typical questions might include:

- Would the users like to work with the same project team again?
- How could the project results have been more useful?
- How could the project results have been more sustainable?
- How has the customer's capacity increased through use of project deliverables?
- Are project team members more loyal to the parent company?
- How have project team members improved their capabilities?
- What organizational learning has occurred?
- What new technology and methods has the company developed?

# TriHealth Case to Determine Sponsor Responsibilities

## Ending Example

TriHealth defined the role of project sponsors and used a four-stage life cycle model to describe what sponsors need to perform at each stage in the project life cycle. TriHealth also defined other roles such as project leader, performance improvement consultant, core team member, and subject matter expert. To make it easier for the executives to learn their role as sponsor, several standards were developed, such as charters and a project tracking tool along with instructions and training. TriHealth is making good progress, but realizes it is a never-ending journey to help their sponsors keep improving. The sponsor role definitions and an example mini-charter used by TriHealth are shown below followed by lessons they have learned.

## Project Executive Sponsor Role

Initiating Stage

- Empower project leader with well-defined charter, which is the overarching guide
- Clearly define expected outcomes
- Demonstrate commitment to and prioritization of project
- Define decision-making methods and responsibility—sponsor/project leader/team
- Partner with project leader to identify obstacles, barriers, and silos to overcome.

Planning Stage

- Ensure project leader understands business context for organization
- Ensure project leader develops overall project plan
- Assist project leader in developing vertical and horizontal communication plan
- Demonstrate personal interest in project by investing time and energy needed
- Secure necessary resources and organizational support

Executing Stage

- Communicate and manage organizational politics
- Visibly empower and support project leader vertically and horizontally
- Build relationships with key stakeholders
- Actively listen to and promote team and project to stakeholders
- Remove obstacles and ensure progress of project
- Ensure goals are met and stakeholders are satisfied.

Closing Stage

- Ensure closure; planned completion or termination
- Ensure results and lessons learned are captured and shared
- Ensure assessment of related applications or opportunities
- Ensure any necessary next steps are assigned and resourced
- Recognize contributions and celebrate completion
- Negotiate follow-up date(s) to assess project status.

## Mini Project Charter

Outpatient Angioplasty
April, 2010

### Business Case

For the past year at Hospital A, there has been an increase in the volume of Radial Angioplasty procedures under the care of Dr. Smith and Dr. Jones. Hospital A has begun marketing this procedure to the community, which will further increase the volumes.

Radial angioplasty has gained recognition as being safer, less invasive, and with fewer complications. Postoperative vascular

*(Continued)*

complications are significantly fewer, enabling the patient to have a speedier and easier recovery. Inpatient hospitalization is usually not required, making it more economical.

Currently at Hospital A, all patients scheduled for an angioplasty (radial or femoral) are admitted to inpatient after the procedure. Hospital A is not currently set up to manage angioplasty cases as out-patients. CMS (Medicare) does not reimburse for inpatient stay after radial angioplasty, without complications and other co-morbidities.

### Project Scope

This project will focus upon treating scheduled (nonemergent) radial angioplasty patients in the safest, least restrictive environment after their procedure. The goal is to design a treatment program that focuses on the patient returning home the same day after an uncomplicated angioplasty procedure. Patient safety, patient value, and evidence-based medicine will drive the design of the outpatient angioplasty services future state.

**Milestone Schedule:** *List key accomplishments that show progression of the project quality*

*Table 3.7. Milestone Schedule*

| Milestone | Estimated date for completion | Responsible party | Com-pleted date |
|---|---|---|---|
| | (start date) | | |
| Define current state angio-plasty practices at Hospital A | March 2011 | Director and angioplasty team | March 2011 |
| Determine financial implications around reimbursement and denials | April 2011 | Director and team | April 2011 |
| Define critical elements for outpatient angioplasty program | April 2011 | Angioplasty team | April 2011 |
| Design future state for angioplasty treatment in the outpatient setting | April 2011 | Angioplasty team | April 2011 |
| Complete final report and present to the council | May 2011 | Director and Dr. Smith | May 2011 |

*(Continued)*

**Potential Risks** *Things that could impact projected project process and outcomes*

1. Physician and staff buy-in
2. Patient and family expectations
3. Capital expenditures for future state—staffing, equipment, etc.
4. Financial impact on revenues of same day discharges.

**Key Stakeholders** *Individuals or departments who are involved in the project process or outcomes, whose interest may be positively or negatively affected by the project, or whose support is necessary for project success*

1. Cardiologists
2. Cath Lab staff
3. Care Management
4. Angio suite staff
5. Telemetry
6. Patient Placement Services
7. Revenue Management
8. Patients and families.

**Resources Required to Achieve Desired Outcomes** *Funding, people, equipment/supplies, or facilities required for the project activity and implementation*

Several team meetings to be scheduled to address the design and implementation for the future state for the treatment of post procedure angioplasty outpatients.

| Initiation approvals | | Completion approvals |
|---|---|---|
| | Sponsor signature/dept/date | |
| | Project leader signature/dept/date | |

(Continued)

### Lessons Learned

Project leaders and sponsors need to make a concerted effort to remind each other that the chartering process is a negotiated process between the team and sponsor and time needs to be built in for this process.

It is easy to fall back into old habits of drafting charters and just getting sponsor sign off. All parties need to hold each other accountable to use the new process.

The process of negotiating the charter content between the team and the sponsor provides both the buy-in from the team and a better clarity on what the sponsor wants achieved.

The sponsor also has a better idea of the depth of the project and resources required based on the questions that are fielded during the chartering process.

Providing this ability to understand more fully the project intent decreases the need for re-clarification once the project is already progressing and can avoid rework and delays.

Linda Galvin, RN, MSN, CMC

Director of Performance Improvement and Consulting

TriHealth Inc.

# How Effective Sponsors Help Achieve the Competing Objectives

### Executives Setting Strategy and Managers Implementing It

The sponsor, by definition, serves as the link between senior management and the project team. In that capacity, he can repeatedly emphasize how the project fits in the larger organizational goals. Sponsors often help select project managers and then the sponsor and project manager serve as a team. Early in the project, sponsors emphasize why the project is important and they typically have many informal conversations so the project manager can, in turn, reinforce project alignment. Sponsors encourage project managers to solve problems at their own level when practical, but serve as a ready escalation point. If the project is not working out or no longer needed, sponsors can lead any possible termination decision.

### Sustainable Organizational Capability and Achieving Current Business Results

One of a sponsor's overarching responsibilities is to deliver results. The results often provide both current business benefits and increasing future capability. Sponsors reinforce how the project fits in the big picture of organizational goals—current and future. In the project charter sponsors insist that a project team look at lessons from previous projects to perform better on the project that is just starting. Sponsors also insist that lessons be derived near the end of a project and fed back into the system so future projects will be better planned and managed.

### Project Goals and Operational Goals

Part of a sponsor's duty is to help select the project manager and to provide the needed resources to successfully complete the project. In both of these actions, sponsors need to actively consider the other work of the organization's portfolio. This consideration includes prioritizing the project in the context of the entire organization. Sponsors develop effective relationships with many stakeholders including those who run the organization's ongoing operations.

### One Function's Goals and Another Function's Goals

The sponsor serves as a link between the customer and the project team whether the customer is external or internal. Sponsors often establish relationships with peers in other functions so they will support the project, but also to help ensure they receive the desired results. Sponsors ensure that the transition of deliverables from the project team to the operational users is smooth.

# Top 10 Assessment Questions

1. How are sponsors selected and trained in your company?
2. How do sponsors interact with other executives?
3. What is the overall job description for sponsors?
4. How is project success defined and at what points is it measured?
5. What do sponsors do during project selection?
6. What do sponsors do during project initiating?
7. What do sponsors do during project planning?
8. What do sponsors do during the executing stage?
9. What do sponsor do during the closing stage?
10. What do sponsors do during the leveraging benefits stage?

# CHAPTER 4

# Leading Project Managers: The Project Executive Role

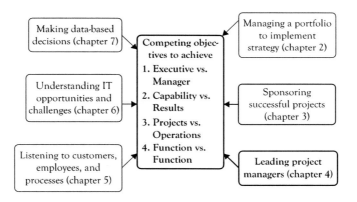

Often, an executive has one or more project managers reporting to her. This chapter describes what project managers do and how an executive oversees their efforts. Specifically, how is it both similar and different to lead a project manager instead of a functional manager? While there are many definitions of leadership, we focus on the process of establishing a vision and then strategizing, aligning, communicating, and motivating people to achieve that vision.[1] The purpose of this chapter is to help you:

- Determine the specific duties project managers need to perform in your organization,
- Describe the personal leadership you need to coach your project manager direct reports, and
- Describe the tasks need to perform as you lead your project manager direct report.

## Messer Case to Lead Project Managers

Founded in 1932, Messer is a full-service complex commercial construction company specializing in building for health care, higher education, and life sciences. For many years at Messer Construction Company, we observed the performance of Project Managers and were challenged by the fact that while they were achieving high results, results would vary from one project to the next. This cyclical pattern didn't follow typical logic in that since the Project Manager had gained more experience on the previous project, he should be able to apply that experience at a higher level and achieve higher results on subsequent projects. The challenge is that with this variation in results, it is far more difficult to predict outcomes that would accomplish a consistent and successful project and overall company business plan. Our interest then became a study of what causes variation in performance.

**The key question Messer Construction leaders faced** is how can they effectively lead their project managers in efforts to consistently complete successful projects? This is the classic question regarding leadership of project managers and the subject of this chapter.

## Project Executives

A project executive supervises one or more project managers as direct reports and is coresponsible for delivering project results with the sponsor and project manager. He provides functional resources, governs methods used on the project, helps the PM develop, and delivers project results according to plan. Ideally, a project executive would have experience as a project manager and would serve on the leadership team. Lacking these experiences, it would be helpful to enlist the ear of an experienced project manager for advice as needed. This experienced project manager could be an internal expert or hired from outside the organization. Effective project executives can anticipate criticism as various stakeholders hold differing opinions and are well-served by having a thick skin.

While much guidance has been written for supervisors generally, there is very little standardization of what a project executive should do. What is written generally overlaps with the role of sponsor. In this chapter we describe the task and coaching duties an executive needs to perform overall and at each project life cycle stage when serving as the direct supervisor of a project manager. While coaching and task responsibilities are somewhat overlapping, we find it helpful to remind executives that there are some duties they **must do** as well as those to help develop the project manager. If the executive is also serving as sponsor, the responsibilities described in the previous chapter also apply.

# Project Managers

A project manager is an individual who is responsible for leading a team that creates unique products and/or services on a temporary basis to meet the needs of one or more customers subject to constraints of time, money, and other resources. We now introduce two global standards and one rapidly emerging trend that may become a standard in describing the role of project managers.

### Project Manager Standard Definitions

A classic, yet limited definition of the project manager's aims is "to achieve the project objectives."[2] Yet this same global source, the *PMBOK® Guide*, also discusses several responsibilities the project manager must accept in order to achieve the project objectives including:

- Identifying requirements and ensuring the project plan aligns with organizational goals,
- Addressing the needs, concerns, and expectations of stakeholders,
- Balancing the competing project constraints of scope, quality, schedule, budget, resources, and risk,
- Progressively elaborating plans as more detailed and specific information and more accurate estimates become available,
- Controlling assigned project resources, and
- Leading the project team as they ensure the flow of the project and create the project's products.[3]

The standard United Kingdom (UK) source, the Office of Government Commerce (OGC) seeks to operationalize the project manager's role from the UK project management standard (PRINCE2). The PRINCE2 definition of a project manager is "the person given the authority and responsibility to manage the project on a day-to-day basis to deliver the required products within the constraints agreed with the Project Board."[4]

*PMBOK® Guide* and PRINCE2 both use a stage gate model to describe the flow of project work with the need for stage ending deliverables to be accepted and organize a project manager's responsibilities into multiple process groups or themes. The *PMBOK® Guide* has the nine process groups of integration, scope, time, cost, quality, human resources, communications, risk, and procurement.[5] PRINCE2 uses the seven themes of: business case, organization, quality, plans, risks, changes, and progress.[6]

A trend that has proven to be very popular in software development projects and is spreading to some other types of projects is known as agile. Agile project management is an iterative method of determining requirements for development projects. It requires an empowered project team, with frequent supplier and customer input. Agile techniques are best used in small-scale projects or projects that are too complex for the customer to understand and specify before testing prototypes. Project outputs are delivered in small increments every two to four weeks.[7] In an effort to sound truly different, the equivalent of a project manager in an agile environment is called a ScrumMaster. The ScrumMaster is responsible for making sure a team lives by agile values and practices. The ScrumMaster protects the team by making sure they do not over-commit themselves. The ScrumMaster facilitates daily meetings and becomes responsible for removing any obstacles that are brought up by the team during those meetings.[8]

*PMBOK® Guide* and PRINCE2 are both widely accepted standards that use a process driven, planning approach. Agile, which is rapidly gaining popularity, uses a reactive, emergent approach. Since it is difficult or impossible to fully plan many projects at the outset, many organizations are experimenting with parts of the agile philosophy and methods that can be used with the more traditional approaches.

*Applied Project Manager Definition for this Book*

In this book, we will primarily use the larger global standard (*PMBOK®*
*Guide*) with ideas and techniques from the other two approaches. In
short, a project manager leads a team in developing an understanding
of the customers needs and desires (often in an iterative fashion). The
project manager is responsible for delivering products and/or services
that will satisfy those needs and desires, subject to constraints, risks,
and to managing changes that may come from customers or other
sources.

Stage-by-stage responsibilities for both project executives and project managers are outlined in Table 4.1. In the following section we
describe what project managers need to do at each point in the project
life so the executive who leads them can understand their duties. The
final major section of this chapter describes the responsibilities of
project executives.

# Project Manager Responsibilities by Project Stage

We now describe what a project manager needs to do at each point in
the project to better understand the demands of an executive who has a
project manager direct report.

## Project Manager Overarching Responsibilities

When considering overall project responsibilities, a project manager
needs to remember how project success is determined. Satisfying customers is most important, followed by meeting agreements (according
to specifications, on time, and on budget), and finally achieving broader
organizational and team benefits.

First, a project manager has to satisfy the project's primary customers.
On some projects this is best accomplished by creating exactly the deliverables that were agreed to initially and delivering them when promised,
for the agreed amount of resources. On other projects, business conditions and customers' desires change considerably. On those projects, the
project manager needs to work very closely with customers to understand

*Table 4.1. Project Manager and Project Executive Stage-by-Stage Responsibilities*

| Stage | Project manager (PM) responsibilities | Project executive (PE) task responsibilities | PE coaching responsibilities |
|---|---|---|---|
| Overarching | Satisfy customers, deliver promised results on time & on budget, support team decisions, manage communications, champion project | Oversee PM, Provide resources, Provide subject area decision-making and continuity, lead improvement within functional area | Empower and promote PM, help PM with leadership, communications, and "big picture" understanding, help PM with project team, leadership team, sponsor, and stakeholders, balance quality and urgency focus |
| Selecting | Help identify and justify rationale for potential projects | Participate in project selection (if member of leadership team) | Coach PM to identify and justify rationale for potential projects |
| Initiating | Write charter rough draft with team, negotiate charter with sponsor | Recommend direct report to be selected as PM, Help PM develop business case for project, work with sponsor on business case as needed | Help PM understand requirements, help PM understand charter concept and methods, help PM incorporate lessons learned from previous projects |
| Planning | Create plans for communications, scope, schedule, budget, and project team | Set project expectations, ensure PM creates needed plans | Help PM define requirement, and schedule, help PM align various goals and develop culture, Progressively delegate |
| Executing | Acquire, develop, and lead project team, manage risks and changes, monitor, control, and report progress | Provide continuing direction, attend progress meetings, personally engage stakeholders as needed | Advise PM on achieving and reporting progress, help PM replan |
| Closing | Transition project deliverables to users, capture lessons learned, evaluate team members, administratively close project | Ensure lessons learned are captured and disseminated, evaluate project manager, sign off on project closure | Ensure stakeholders are satisfied; Help PM assess team members, Help PM understand importance of and disseminate lessons learned |
| Leveraging benefits | Schedule and conduct follow-up assessment | Participate in (or at least insist on) follow-up assessment | Coach PM on conducting follow-up |

their need for changes, help the customer understand the impact of the changes on the project schedule and budget, and then make the changes the customer desires. The project manager is then expected to deliver the revised deliverables according to any agreed upon revisions in the schedule and budget.

Project managers facilitate teams through meetings that often include a series of thought expansion (when exploring options) and focusing (when selecting approaches) efforts. To do this, they:

- Ask questions,
- Establish order out of chaos,
- Create detailed and unified project plans, and
- Think many times and then act decisively.[9]

The project manager needs to support team decisions, champion the project, and manage project communications. Often, project team members will have differing opinions. The project manager needs to ensure all opinions are heard, and decisions are made with qualitative and quantitative data. Once decisions are made, all project team members need to support the decisions so the project team speaks with one voice. The project manager typically spends a large amount of time advocating for the project by communicating with many stakeholders.

### Project Manager Selecting Stage Responsibilities

The project manager sometimes participates in project selection by helping to identify possible projects and justifying the rationale for each. At many organizations, all employees are encouraged to propose possible projects consistent with organizational goals. The person who proposes a project and/or another person who will be the likely project manager will often need to compile brief justification regarding why the project should be selected. Essentially, the leadership team makes investment decisions with projects. They decide if the expected project benefits (discounted for risks) appear to be worth the investment in cash and other resources needed to complete the project.

### Project Manager Initiating Stage Responsibilities

The project manager's main responsibilities during initiating are to lead the team in developing a draft charter and then negotiate it with the sponsor to authorize the project. As we have emphasized, one of the most important project management documents is the charter. The charter is a high-level project plan. Both the typical contents and process of developing charters are described in chapter 3. Sponsors have more organizational power than project managers, but the charter should still be negotiated. The project manager needs to express his strongly held opinions on approach and feasibility. At the end of the negotiation, both sponsor and project manager should be in agreement on all portions of the charter and feel it is realistic.

### Project Manager Planning Stage Responsibilities

Much of the detail work in this stage is performed by the project manager, core team, subject matter experts, and other project stakeholders. Each of the detailed planning documents is an elaboration of a short statement contained in the project charter. The level of detail can vary considerably depending on the project size, risk, and complexity. This work includes developing the plans for communications, scope, schedule, budget, and project team.

### Project Communications Planning

Many projects fail because of inadequate communications. The purpose of a communications plan is to more fully understand:

- Who all of the project stakeholders are?
- How they are prioritized?
- What each wants from the project?
- What information each needs to share with the project team?
- What information each needs to receive from the project team?
- The most effective means of receiving and acting appropriately upon the received information, and
- When each communication needs to be received?

The short answer to the project communications challenge is not to just copy everyone on every communication, but to carefully target communications. Project managers often discover that various stakeholders have some of the same communication needs. In these cases, the project manager can simplify the communications by using some of the same communications for these groups.

## Project Scope Planning

The project manager and team then ask each stakeholder what their requirements are for the project. These requirement lists are often quite long and contradictory, so prioritization decisions need to be made—often with the help of the sponsor and/or project executive. On some projects the requirements for the entire project can be determined at the outset, on other projects the team decides to plan the early part of the project in detail right away and plan future portions as results from early parts provide additional detail that help with the later planning.

In either case, the requirements are then normally used to create a work breakdown structure (WBS). The WBS is an outline of all of the deliverables that will be created on the project, broken down into fine enough detail so the work to create each can be accurately estimated, and one person can be held accountable to both plan and create each deliverable.

## Project Schedule Planning

Project schedules can be tricky as they may be limited by any or all of the following five factors:

1. The logical order in which activities must be completed,
2. The time for each activity,
3. The availability of key workers when needed,
4. Imposed dates and
5. Cash flow.[10]

Creating workable project schedules requires the project manager to use both specific methods (science) and judgment (art). We now briefly describe each step. After the product deliverables are understood, the project manager and team can estimate the schedule. This begins by determining the work activity needed to produce each deliverable identified in the WBS. Once the activities are understood, they can be sequenced by asking what can begin immediately, what can begin next, etc. Teams often write one activity per sticky note and place them on a work surface so the team can debate the most logical order.

The project manager and team need to estimate how long each work activity will take to complete. This should be done by envisioning who will do the work, what is involved, and what other commitments the workers have. The duration estimates for each activity can then be combined with the logical order already determined to estimate a possible schedule. This first cut at a schedule may be too long, in which case the logical order and/or the duration of individual activities need to be reconsidered. This first cut schedule, however, may actually need to be lengthened when worker availability, imposed dates (such as fiscal year demands), and cash flow are considered.

## Project Budget Planning

A project budget can be developed from the schedule. Each work activity needs to be estimated at whatever rate per hour the worker costs. Many work products also require materials, equipment, and other expenses. Once the total project costs are forecast, they need to be put in a cash flow according to the schedule. At that point, it is possible that the cash flow coming in may limit how rapidly project expenses can be paid out— thereby slowing the project progress.

## Project Team Planning

Upon first hearing of a potential project, a project manager begins to assemble a small core team who will ideally be with him throughout the process, helping with work and decisions. If the project has much size, however, the project manager often needs a larger team at key points in time. As more planning details are determined, the need for more workers, especially those with a particular expertise, begins to emerge. A project manager will identify those needs and identify where those workers might be –whether internal to the company or hired from outside. While project managers often negotiate directly, if every department only offers unproven workers, a project manager may need help from either sponsor or project executive to secure the promise of at least some experienced staff.

### Project Manager Executing Stage Responsibilities

In this section, we focus on the project manager responsibilities that occur when the project team is executing work to satisfy the agreed upon requirements. These responsibilities include working with the project team, risks and changes, progress, and results.

### Acquire, Develop, and Lead Project Team

Acquiring the needed workers often starts during the project planning when the need for particular expertise is identified. Depending upon how much authority was granted to the project manager in the charter, they may need help in securing the services of some workers who are in high demand.

Remembering that the most important project success criteria are satisfying customers and delivering on promises, one might think that developing a project team is of less importance. However, developing both individual team members and the project team as a whole is important both to accomplish the work of the project and to groom workers for more responsibility. The best project managers see projects as ideal training grounds for worker development.

When leading a project team, project managers need to realize that contemporary project management is integrative, iterative, and collaborative. Projects are integrative, as many parts need to come together into a coherent whole. They are iterative, since results of early work lead to and constrain choices for later work. They are collaborative, since many diverse stakeholders need to be accommodated and many diverse team members need to work together.[11] Other than on some small projects, the project manager has neither all of the answers nor the capability of personally getting them. Various team members need to step up in their respective areas. Project managers generally find an empowering style of leadership is more effective than a controlling style of management, yet the project manager is responsible for overall project results.

## Manage Risks and Changes

The project manager normally leads the team through risk identification, assessment, and response planning when creating the project charter. The project manager needs to make sure that the person who was assigned responsibility for each major risk during chartering continually monitors for indicators that the risk event may be coming and starts the response plan if appropriate. On many of the larger risks, the project manager is the person responsible for these actions. Typical responses to negative risks (threats) either attempt to lower the probability of the risk event from occurring or lower the impact to the project if the risk event does occur. Conversely, typical responses to positive risks (opportunities) either increase the probability of the event occurring or further capitalize upon the results if it does occur. Additionally, the project manager should periodically lead the team in efforts to uncover new risk events that were not originally foreseen, but may occur due to changing circumstances.

Change is inevitable on many projects. In fact, the agile school of thought suggests it is so difficult on many projects to plan the entire project, that only very high-level plans are made initially and detailed plans are developed every two to four weeks to determine possible progress. This allows many changes to be incorporated. At the other extreme, on some projects the entire plan is approved and every possible change needs to be proposed, evaluated, decided upon, and if approved included in a revised project plan. Regardless of the tolerance for change, the project manager needs to ensure that any agreed upon change is incorporated into all planning and control and any unapproved change does not creep into the project.

## Monitor, Control, and Report Progress

Project managers monitor both their personal work and that of their team. The style of monitoring can vary from informal management by walking around on small projects with workers geographically close, to formalized reports on larger projects and/or those that may be dispersed geographically. The level of detail and frequency a project manager needs to monitor is often much more precise than what she, in turn, reports to sponsors and customers.

Control is established by having a plan and comparing the monitored progress against the plan. When the difference between plan and actual (called variance) is too great, the project manager acts to get progress back on track. Again, this can range from an informal conversation with a team member as they brainstorm alternatives, to formalized direction.

Customers and sponsors want to know that progress is being made. Project managers and teams do not want to be micro-managed. The way to satisfy both is to have a standard method and timing for reporting progress. One way to envision this is to consider three time periods: the immediate past (since the last report), the current (until the next report), and the remainder until project conclusion. The report may include the following:

- **Immediate Past Period**
  - Plan as approved for that time period
  - Actual progress made during that time period
  - Variance between actual and plan
  - Reasons for any variances.

- **Current Period until Next Report**
  - Current plan including any approved changes
  - Risks likely to occur during this time.

- **Remaining Period until Project Conclusion**
  - Plan until conclusion
  - Risks likely to occur during this time.[12]

Deliver Results

The reason a project is conducted is that some customer wants the resulting deliverables. Therefore, the most important responsibility for a project manager is to deliver results that the customers can use. One of the great contributions of agile thinking in projects is the concept of incremental benefits. This means the customer should not need to wait until project conclusion to receive any benefits from the project. To the extent possible (it is easier on some types of projects than others), the project manager should deliver drafts, prototypes, partial products, information, or other interim deliverables as soon as possible to help the customer realize some gain from the project early. Regardless of how many incremental benefits are possible the project manager is primarily accountable for delivering any results that have been promised. That means all of the work with the team, risks, quality, and reporting are merely means to help ensure the project will deliver results.

### Project Manager Closing Stage Responsibilities

During the closing stage project managers transition project deliverables to users, evaluate team members and provide input to their performance reports, capture and share lessons learned, and administratively close the project.

Project managers often use a checklist to make sure all deliverables have been accepted by users and all needed support has been included. This often means including instructions, warrantees, training, or other support. Since the most important measure of project success is customer satisfaction, merely transitioning deliverables, without the ability to use them, is not wise.

Project managers often do not formally evaluate team members—their functional managers do. Project managers can do two things to lessen the potential negative impact of this. First, they need to continually keep functional managers informed and eager to see the project succeed. Given other demands on the functional manager, this is not always easy. Second, project managers can provide unsolicited input to the functional manager regarding the performance of team members. If the team member spent a large amount of time on the project and the input is well-written, specific, and reasonable, a busy functional manager may be tempted to use it in the performance review. Project managers can tell their team members that they will be providing input to the performance evaluations.

The project manager often works with the sponsor to secure lessons learned as described in sponsor responsibilities in the previous chapter. At this point, the project manager needs to formally close the project with all workers and resources reassigned as appropriate.

### Project Manager Leveraging Benefits Stage Responsibilities

The leveraging stage is for an assessment of how well the end-users of the project deliverables are able to use them. Were the benefits that were promised during project selection delivered? Has the client capability improved because of the project deliverables and has the company capability improved because of utilizing lessons learned from the project process? Have any methods developed on the project been reused on other projects and have any project results been used in additional ways beyond the immediate project results? The project manager needs to schedule and conduct a follow-up assessment to ascertain which of the promised benefits have been realized.

## Project Executive Responsibilities by Project Stage

The first part of this chapter described what a project manager needs to do at each stage of the project life cycle. The remainder of the chapter deals with what an executive needs to do when a project manager directly reports to her. While some of these things can be delegated to others such as a sponsor or a human resources person, the executive a project manager reports directly to needs to ensure these leadership responsibilities are accomplished. These are responsibilities typically of an executive who a project manager reports directly to—not of a sponsor as described in the previous chapter. We focus specifically on how to lead a project manager. Some of this is just a difference in emphasis in comparison to leading a functional manager or individual contributor, but much is unique to leading project managers. At each project stage we describe both task and coaching responsibilities for the project executive.

## Project Executive Overarching Responsibilities

The sponsor has primary responsibility for directing a project, the project manager has primary responsibility for managing the project, but the project manager's supervisor has responsibility to oversee the project manager as the results of the project reflect on her part of the organization. Sometimes it can be a delicate dance to work effectively with a sponsor who has differing goals.

## Lead in Functional Area

A project executive often has functional responsibilities within the company. She is responsible for decision-making within that function. For instance, an engineering manager is responsible for how engineering is conducted. The project executive provides continuity and spearheads improvement within her area. The project executive also directly supervises the project manager.

This executive needs to commit the necessary resources from her division to the project. Often the project manager does not have personal authority to commit resources. Many projects also require resources from other parts of the organization. It is the project manager's primary responsibility to secure those resources, but both sponsors and supervisors can be helpful.

An executive may have both project managers and functional managers as direct reports. Some performance criteria may be the same for both. This forms the cohesive bond between the two groups. Typical common project-specific performance goals may include items such as:

- Milestone completion on time and with acceptable quality,
- Customer satisfaction,
- Budgeted cost versus actual cost, and
- Project on-time completion.

Performance goals such as these directly help to achieve current business success. More challenging is developing appropriate and easily measured goals for helping to develop the long-term capability of the firm. While long-term organizational growth is more often considered by functional managers, it can be fostered by also including project manager specific performance goals such as:

- Realization of promised benefits,
- Reuse of portions of the project plan and/or results,
- Development, retention, and promotions of team members, and
- Reapplication of lessons developed during the project.[13]

## Help the Project Manager Communicate Effectively

Projects typically have many diverse stakeholders and a variety of team members from differing backgrounds. Projects often have significant time pressures. Finally, many projects create products or services that in turn force significant and not always understood change. All of these combine to make communications more important and more challenging. Project managers spend large portions of their time communicating one way or another. Two analogies that may help are to consider the project manager as both a bridge and a ladder. Project managers need to bridge gaps in understanding between various stakeholders and various team members. Project managers also need to serve as ladders, providing a structure to keep the project making progress. Effective communications help project managers in both their bridge and ladder roles.

Leading in a manner that enhances cross-functional integration helps with incorporating the various stakeholder needs in planning, in making timely decisions, and progressing well. One critical communication channel in this process is between you and the project manager who reports directly to you. To the extent you can have frequent, rapid, and candid conversations, you set the stage for the project manager to have the same kind of communications with a myriad of others.

Project executives often encourage managers to develop standard approaches or even templates for communication needs such as:

- Project elevator pitch to briefly describe what the project is and why it is important,
- Project charter to authorize the project,

- Stakeholder register to list, prioritize, and describe needs of each stakeholder,
- Communications matrix to outline who needs to know what, when, and by what means,
- Risk register to outline major risks with strategy to handle each and who is responsible,
- Progress reports to help key stakeholders understand progress and challenges, and
- Customer feedback to understand how users feel about both the project methods and results.

## Empower the Project Manager

Project managers often enjoy little position power because they often have few if any direct reports. This means they cannot order something to be done, but have to persuade others to perform. Leaders can encourage project managers to develop other forms of power such as:

- Referent power based upon establishing personal relationships,
- Expert power based upon knowledge and skills, and
- Connection power based on relationships with important people such as sponsors.[14]

Project managers need to develop a deep understanding of various stakeholders. Managing stakeholder relations is a key part of any project manager's duties and should be assessed. Completing a project on time, on budget, and to specification is of less value if important stakeholders are ignored or treated poorly. The sponsor and leadership team are particularly important stakeholders. A project executive does her project manager a great service when he helps the project manager plan for meetings with these critical stakeholders. The project executive also needs to help the project manager handle informal interactions with many powerful stakeholders—effectively navigating political reality.

Another project-specific skill is to quickly lead her new team to develop a common understanding of the upcoming project and then negotiate it with a sponsor and possibly other key individuals. This requires the ability to:

- Understand projects are investments,
- Think in big pictures,
- Integrate various components,
- Envision how the schedule could play out,
- Foresee risks,
- Understand people (the project team, sponsor, and key stakeholders), and
- Be willing to suggest the project may be a nonstarter if the risks are too high.

A special opportunity sometimes arises with project managers. Some project managers are very experienced. If you have one of these individuals reporting to you, consider how you can capitalize upon some of their expertise in mentoring more junior project managers.

## Develop the Project Manager

We described project manager responsibilities in the early part of this chapter, both on an overall basis and a stage-by-stage basis. Many of these responsibilities are similar to those faced by functional managers, such as satisfying customers, ensuring work is completed on time and to acceptable quality, leading a team, etc. However, a few of the project manager responsibilities differ from those of functional managers, and a leader needs to help the project manager develop the project-specific competencies such as dealing with stakeholders, charters, schedules, and replanning.

Projects often have aggressive timelines. The entire reason projects are undertaken if someone wants to use the deliverables that will be created and sooner is better than later. That said, executives can be most effective when leading with an appropriate sense of urgency balanced by an insistence on quality. This does not mean setting unrealistic expectations. It does mean a continual focus on delivering useful results in a timely manner.

Leading in an empowering style often sets project managers and others free to make quick decisions and keep making rapid progress.

Projects are especially good vehicles for progressively delegating more responsibility. An executive can work closely with the project manager at the outset to help ensure the project gets off to a good start. As the project manager proves he understands the big picture of where the project fits and what is most critical to key stakeholders, more and more detail and visibility can be given to the project manager. By encouraging the project manager to empower core team members, the project manager will have more capacity for higher level decision-making.

The last portion, and perhaps most important, in personally leading a project manager is to always have the goal of retaining and even promoting the project manager for the future. This implies continually keeping an eye open for development opportunities, but also trying to help the project manager have a sense that he wants to remain at your company. This may include both monitoring the project manager's feelings and promoting advantages of staying with the company.

## Project Executive Selecting Stage Responsibilities

The project executive, like all other employees, needs to identify potential projects that may help to further the organization's strategic plan. The executive can best do this by understanding the strategic direction of the firm and the selection criteria for projects. Additionally, if the executive is part of the leadership team, he will actively participate in deciding which projects to select.

The project executive also needs to coach her direct reports on how to identify potential projects and justify the rationale for each. This coaching on how to write very brief business cases will serve the project manager well. Project managers need to be able to briefly describe what a project involves and why it is important. Project managers need to actively promote their project to many audiences at many levels.

## Project Executive Initiating Stage Responsibilities

Project executives need to carefully recommend which of their direct reports might be appropriate to manage a specific project. Projects are great training grounds, but everyone is not a good choice for every project either as the project manager or in other roles. Leading a person who is not a good choice for their respective role is difficult.

Projects are typically initiated (made official) by a signed charter. The most essential element of a charter is the business case. Project executives can help their project managers develop compelling business cases by getting them to consider three questions. First, how is the project strategically aligned to one or more company goals? Second, what is the return on investment of time and money? Third, what is the emotional hook that will convince members of the leadership team to select the project and will convince the project team and other stakeholders to persevere through tough spots?

Part of the wisdom a seasoned executive hopefully brings is an adaptive style based upon lessons learned from previous projects. Role-modeling the adoption of what worked well in the past and how to change things that worked poorly sends a clear message to project managers that they need to do the same. Managers who do not use lessons learned keep repeating previous mistakes and inefficiencies. Part of leading in an adaptive style is also being flexible. No two projects are exactly alike and flexibility within normal good practice and procedures is essential.

Projects are performed to satisfy a need. Requirements gathering sessions are often conducted to elicit needs and wants from various stakeholders. While more in-depth requirements gathering will occur during planning, a project executive helps her project manager by insisting that high-level requirements be determined as early as possible.

## Project Executive Planning Stage Responsibilities

Project executives can help project managers have more stature by visibly supporting them. Setting clear expectations and delegating to the project manager by stages both let the project manager understand exactly how much authority he has, thereby increasing his confidence. Executives can lead project managers by exception. That is, the project manager can lead his team in the manner he wishes (subject to ethical standards and any mandatory policies and procedures) as long as the progress and results are within a stipulated tolerance. Once the performance exceeds the tolerance, the executive can dictate.

Once a project manager understands the wants and needs of the myriad stakeholders, it is time to prioritize them. She needs to make tradeoffs such as determining what features and functions will not be included, which stakeholder demands are met first, or when schedule or budget demands are loosened to allow more scope—or vice versa. As an executive with a big picture view of the organization, you can help ensure the project manager makes sensible tradeoff decisions.

A special case of stakeholder alignment is the members of the project team—both core team and subject matter experts. A project executive can encourage their project manager to have one-on-one discussions with each member to understand their personal goals. Often those can be factored into the assignment of specific duties on the project. Effective project managers try to align personal goals with project goals to the extent possible.

A project-specific skill is creating and managing project schedules. Developing realistic project schedules is an iterative activity that takes into account many factors. A project executive helps her project manager by imposing as few arbitrary dates as possible and working with the project manager to resolve key worker availability and cash flow issues.

The project manager has primary goals of satisfying customers and delivering project results as promised. However, the company benefits more if project managers also help to groom team members for greater responsibility. Projects have a culture just as organizations do. You can encourage the project manager to develop a project culture that gives team members confidence to offer ideas, make decisions, and take action. An empowering project culture makes it easier for the project manager to develop team members. As the team members develop specific project competencies, the project manager has more confidence in them.

### *Project Executive Executing Stage Responsibilities*

Project executives need to provide continuing direction. They can demonstrate how to use balance when intervening. On most projects, there will be times when everything is not going well. A seasoned project executive often develops a sense for when apparent failure partway through a project really is a danger signal and when it represents acceptable progress. When it appears a project is in trouble, you may want to intervene rapidly and aggressively to demonstrate your sense of urgency. On the other hand, you may want to intervene more cautiously and carefully to emphasize how you are empowering the project manager.

You will also want to help your project managers develop a feel for when to let their team members or other stakeholders work and when to intervene. By encouraging the project manager to monitor both team members' motivations and their ongoing morale, it will be easier for him to determine when to intervene.

Project executives can discuss an escalation process with their project managers before it needs to be used. Project managers have more confidence when they understand the limits on the type, size, and timing of issues they can personally decide versus those that need to be escalated.

Timely and clear communication also gives project managers confidence and authority to make decisions when needed. Helping the project manager understand when she needs to wait for more information and when she needs to make a rapid decision also empowers her. As the project manager performs well, showing that you have confidence in her and giving her more authority to make bigger decisions continues the empowerment process. Having the project manager capture, share, and use lessons learned to better manage provides more knowledge and confidence.

Since many project schedules are critically important, it may be necessary to quickly remove a project manager who is not performing. It is often necessary to replace a project manager more rapidly than a functional manager.

Hopefully, the sponsor has ensured that quality measures are described for each milestone. The project executive can be helpful in focusing efforts on those quality measures. As the project progresses, the project executive will often observe how the project manager keeps track of and deals with:

- Ongoing issues that will need to be settled when time and/or information permit,
- Risks that increase or decrease in probability and sometimes occur,

- Proposed changes to the project that need to be approved or not and include in plans, and
- Project communications that can enhance or detract from performance.

Sometimes, the project manager's supervisor will attend project reviews or meet with customers to listen to the voices of customers, employees, and processes. This allows the executive to:

- Show support for the project manager,
- Provide ongoing direction to help the project manager stay aligned with higher level goals,
- Suggest possible improvements to the project process or results (as long as those changes do not adversely impact project priorities),
- Consider opportunities for the larger organization to gain in new ways from the project, and
- Recommend anything up to and including project cancellation so the company does not throw good money after bad in a losing cause.

Project executives may need to have their project manager replan. Replanning skills start with the project manager having workable methods for managing issues, risks, and changes. Strong project managers develop the ability to track cost and schedule in a timely and accurate manner and then the courage to report both honestly. When a project needs to get back on schedule, the project manager may need to take actions to reduce the project scope, overlap sequential activities, temporarily increase workload of individuals, or acquire additional workers. At the extreme, a project may truly be failing and the project manager either needs to rescue it by extreme means or suggest terminating it. Any of these may require approval from the sponsor and/or other key stakeholders.

When you have a project manager reporting to you, insisting that they use standard approaches and templates will help them to control information and help you to have confidence in them. Meeting management can be a particular communication challenge to project managers.

Meetings are important as key decisions get made and lots of expensive staff time is tied up in them. Project managers can be more effective in meeting management if they use:

- Advance agendas to effectively plan each meeting and solicit timely input from stakeholders,
- Minutes to record decisions made, unresolved issues, and action items with responsibilities,
- Issues logs to add any pending decisions and remove those that are resolved, and
- Meeting evaluations so meetings can progressively improve.

### Project Executive Closing Stage Responsibilities

Project executives need to evaluate their project manager direct reports and the end of a project is a natural time for reflection. It is reasonable to partially assess a project manager by how well-managed the project was. A project in trying circumstances could be well-managed and yield mediocre results, while a project in easy circumstances could be poorly managed and still yield good results. A project manager should be partially rewarded based on how well she managed regardless of the challenge faced.

One further challenge project managers often have is that team members are evaluated by the functional manager they report to. Project executives can encourage their project managers to communicate frequently with functional managers and to provide input that may be used in the employee evaluation.

Project executives need to have their project managers ensure stakeholder input is captured and understand how satisfied all of the stakeholders are. It is sometimes difficult to fully satisfy all stakeholders, but project managers need to do their best.

Project executives need to insist that lessons learned are captured and disseminated. Effective use of lessons learned on future projects can help reduce variation. One way to ensure this is to withhold evaluating the project manager and signing off to officially close the project until useful lessons learned are discussed and captured.

### Project Executive Leveraging Benefits Stage Responsibilities

Projects are selected based upon expectation of yielding benefits. Some of the benefits on most projects are impossible to determine until the results have been used for a period. Project executives need to ensure that after the results have been used for an appropriate length of time, the project manager leads a benefits assessment. Several types of questions can be asked. Were the project deliverables as useful as promised? Are any of them able to be reused in different circumstances beyond the original plan? Are any of the methods developed on the project useful in other situations?

## Messer Case to Lead Project Managers

Construction is a service industry. While there is equipment involved in building structures, the work largely is performed by skilled craftsmen lead by effective Project Managers. Senior Project Executives are direct supervisors of Project Managers and, as such, are concerned with both project success and development of Project Managers.

### Lessons Learned

Project executives have found six specific ways to help their project managers learn.

### 1. Align the Project Team

We don't produce our product by trial runs until we get it right, we only get one shot at it. So our attention turns to understanding the complexity of projects and the identification of processes to better assure success. When you look at a typical project, the people assigned to the project are mostly coming together for the first time. The individuals represent many contractors, subcontractors, designers, and the client. As you can imagine, everyone rightfully has their own agenda and goals that they want to achieve, whether that is for their company or for themselves personally. The first challenge is to align these many

*(Continued)*

agendas and goals so they can all be accomplished while assuring a successful completion of a project as defined by the client.

### 2. Achieve Success on Unique Projects

Another dynamic is that this team is building something that has never been built before. As said earlier, each project is widely different than the next, and we get one shot at it. While these two dynamics are alone challenging, the additional forces on the projects are that they need to be completed more safely, faster, for less cost, with high quality and higher overall value—all in an environment that is not typically conducive to the construction process.

### 3. Remove Variation from Project Processes

Given all this, we understand the incredible amount of variation introduced into the process. Management control systems developed over the years have done little to improve project performance because they don't remove variation in the process and typically are lagging indicators of success. The reality is that this is more than managing a process; it is about removing the variation in human performance at the project level where true value is created. Value creation in our industry is done through people. And to the extent a Project Manager can influence the many others in creating this value, the project success will be directly affected. The key to this success is leadership—they ability to influence the outcomes by personally engaging the stakeholders. The primary responsibility of the Senior Project Executive, in leading multiple Project Managers, is to grow their individual leadership abilities.

### 4. Collect Institutional Knowledge

As stated earlier, this is not about implementing more controls. People typically don't respond well to being "controlled." The human spirit, having a passion for what you do and pride in your work, when leveraged, will produce high outcomes and more predictable and consistent results every time. Collectively, our leaders at Messer have more than likely experienced virtually every kind of project challenge; but because of the fragmentation of the construction process, we struggle with leveraging institutional knowledge to improve our individual performance.

*(Continued)*

In solving this, we first needed to find a way to capture this knowledge. In 2003, based on an idea, we created a platform to collect and store our institutional knowledge so that we could share it with leaders across the company. Today we call it our "Center of Excellence." Understanding that evolving technology was going to play a major role in providing access to information, we designed a program to allow all employees in all locations, including remote jobsites, to be able access this knowledge whenever they needed. This form of just-in-time learning radically improved our ability to transfer knowledge—far better than traditional training.

### 5. Share and Use Institutional Knowledge

Structurally, the Center of Excellence is set up primarily like a library, with information arranged by the major divisions of construction work with search capabilities. For each division of work, we identified internal experts who were known for their expertise with this particular type of work. These experts came together and began the process of downloading everything they knew about that work. This is not the content you find in textbooks. This is information that only comes from years of experience. The content includes:

- Best practices
- What to watch out for
- What not to do
- Planning checklists
- Templates
- Outlines
- Pictures
- Videos, and
- Anything that they could share about what worked in creating successful outcomes.

If someone has information they would like to add, they simply forward it to the consultant who reviews it for inclusion. When viewing the content, if someone still had a question or problem that needed further information or insight, the person could click on an icon that would put them directly in contact with the internal experts for that

*(Continued)*

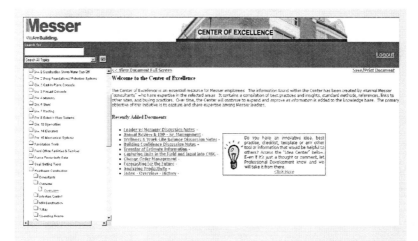

work. We continually add content to the Center of Excellence and are migrating the Center to a more dynamic platform, which will allow everyone to add content without having to channel it all through an administrator.

The next opportunity to ensure Project Managers were performing at the highest level was to find a way to elevate how we share information. The Center of Excellence is one way, but in order to share current issues in a timelier manner, we developed our Best Practices Meetings. From an organizational perspective, each of our nine regions holds a regular "Best Practice" meeting. At this meeting, an agenda drives the sharing of best practices from the company to the region and from the region to the company. Included in this meeting are the region Executive, the Senior Project Executives, and all the Project Managers. Each meeting typically has several predetermined best practices that are presented and discussed, as well as an opportunity for others to share "on the fly." At the bi-weekly Executive meetings, the executives have the opportunity to share best practices from these meetings that they believe should be implemented across the company. Each region leader is then responsible for taking those best practices back to their region to share for implementation. This allows for more expeditious process improvement and greater adoption of the best practice.

*(Continued)*

# Example of Sharing and Utilizing Institutional Knowledge

Messer has for years been the leader of the building construction process focusing on delivering high value to the customer. One element of this value proposition is quality. While we strive to deliver high quality on every project, we are challenged in this effort mainly because a large portion of construction projects are built by many different subcontractors—all who share different definitions of quality. For our Project Managers, the creation and communication of the specific quality expectations for each project is a continual process to assure each subcontractor's definition of quality is consistent with our definition of quality. Over time, we have created many quality plans for the many projects we've built. Within a discussion of best practices, the decision was made that we needed to build further consistency in how communicate, plan, execute, assure and sell quality at Messer. To accomplish this, a quality development team was established to focus creating an overall Messer quality framework as well as the tools necessary to carry out quality construction processes. The elements of the quality system are as follows:

"Quality Leadership System"

1. Quality System Guidelines
2. Project Processes
3. Quality System Administration Tools
4. Building Information Modeling
5. Exterior Building Commissioning
6. Building Systems Commissioning
7. Prefabrication
8. Lean Construction.

The draft of the Quality Leadership System was then presented to the Executive Officers by the quality development team. The result of the presentation was complete buy-in and support for moving forward with this initiative. This is a crucial step, in that each of the Executives is responsible for driving the adoption within her region by all Project Managers on all projects. The implementation plan for

*(Continued)*

the QLS includes the identification of a high-level QLS manager to oversee the QLS and future improvements, pilot projects in each of our nine regions, pilot project feedback on the QLS process plus best practices communicated to a quality steering committee, refinement of the QLS based on the feedback received, establishing quality champions within each of our nine regions to facilitate real-time support, and then company-wide Operations training and implementation on all projects. Beyond Operations, the QLS will be introduced to all corporate support functions to result in a QLS across the entire company.

### 6. Develop Project Manager Leadership and Manage their Careers

As implied earlier, at the core of managing multiple Project Managers is the ability of the Senior Project Executive to personally impact the growth of those leaders. For some years, our performance management process has had well-supported discussions between the Senior Project Executives and Project Managers regarding their line-of-sight goals—for both performance and development. To elevate the process and to ensure greater consistency in performance, individual development planning, and career planning, this year we are implementing a competency-based development process. For each position in the company, a set of competencies are identified and used to create an individual development plan for that person for the next year. As it relates to Project Managers, we leverage the complexities of their specific project as the subject for the goals. Senior Project Executives observe the progress of the Project Manager regularly throughout the year and annually conduct a formal review of progress. Along with these discussions, the Senior Project Executive is able to discuss the next level of competencies for the Project Manager so that they can develop stretch goals that take the Project Manager to the next performance level. The competency-based development process will lead to more consistency in leadership skill sets among Project Managers resulting in more consistent performance.

William S. Krausen

Professional Development Vice President

Messer Construction Co.

# How Leading Project Managers Can Help Achieve Competing Objectives

## Executives Setting Strategy and Managers Implementing It

Executives who have a project manager directly reporting to them focus on project results and continually describe how they are aligned with the company's strategy. They provide continuing direction to the project manager while emphasizing the alignment. Executives who closely follow project progress can continually consider additional ways project results may benefit the company. They ensure timely and clear communication with the project manager, help the project manager understand and manage stakeholder needs, and help the project manager understand how the project is an investment in the company's future.

## Sustainable Organizational Capability and Achieving Current Business Results

Executives who treat the project as a training ground deliver current results and improve the participants. Executives with project manager direct reports personally use and insist the project manager use lessons learned to both improve the current and future projects. They demonstrate to project managers how to use judgment on when to intervene, understanding that quick interventions may lead to current results while delayed interventions may lead to employee development. Executives need to use judgment on replacing the project manager since quickly replacing often yields immediate benefits while a struggling project manager may learn. Effective executives lead the project manager with a goal of keeping and promoting him, establish and use appropriate performance goals, and set clear expectations for the project manager.

## Project Goals and Operational Goals

Executives can simultaneously work toward both project and operational goals by encouraging the project manager to plan for and use open communications with various stakeholders. They can establish some common performance expectations for both project managers and functional managers so they are encouraged to work together. Executives can also encourage their project manager direct reports to provide input to functional managers for possible inclusion in team members' performance reports.

### One Function's Goals and Another Function's Goals

An executive who is the direct supervisor of a project manager can work with the project sponsor to support the project. She can help the project manager communicate effectively with all stakeholders and help the project manager prioritize stakeholder expectations.

## Top 10 Assessment Questions

1. How are your project managers trained to know their specific responsibilities for each stage in a project?
2. What are three to five typical performance expectations you have for project managers in your organization?

How can the executive who has a project manager (direct report) help:

3. The project manager develop personal leadership?
4. Empower the project manager?
5. The project manager to develop project specific competencies?
6. The project manager to communicate effectively?
7. The project manager to be more effective with the project team?
8. The project manager to remove variation from the projects?
9. The project manager collect, share, and use institutional knowledge?
10. The project manager manage their careers?

# CHAPTER 5

# Listening to Customers, Employees, and Processes: A Chief Projects Officer's Role

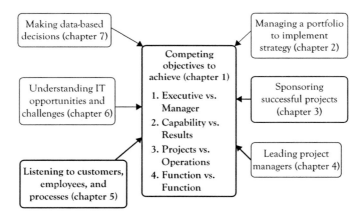

## Chief Projects Officer

The chief projects officer (CPO) is responsible for how projects are conducted in a company. This may include training and mentoring project managers and other people who work on projects. It may include standard approaches to project processes, templates, tools, and metrics. It may include dealing with project customers both internal and external to the organization. It may include building a culture within the organization that helps project managers to become successful. It may include continual improvement of everything associated with management of projects. All of those duties deal with being a competency owner. Sometimes, the facilitation and resource management portions of the leadership team role are combined with this position.

Where can a CPO receive guidance for these various responsibilities? The answer is by listening to the three voices of customers, employees, and processes. The need for this threefold understanding started to emerge from total quality management (TQM) concepts and techniques that began their development in the 1950s and gained prominence in the 1980s. The two widely adopted approaches to TQM today are Malcolm Baldrige and International Organization for Standardization (ISO). In the last 25 years, other approaches have contributed to our knowledge as they expanded upon the quality movement, specifically by helping us operationalize how to deal with the voices. Some of the more useful of these approaches include Voice of the Customer, Employee Engagement, Six Sigma, Lean, and Business Process Management.

The purpose of this chapter is to help you:

- Describe what a CPO would include in a leadership system based upon customers, employees, and processes and why it is so powerful.
- Lead capturing of customer voices and incorporating that knowledge into your portfolio and project management systems.
- Use employee empowerment, engagement, and teamwork in your project management competency.
- Establish and maintain a system and culture of improving your portfolio and project processes.
- Describe how this three-voice system can help you achieve the four competing objectives.

## Midland Case to Improve Performance

The Midland Company began in 1938 as a consumer finance company, expanded into insurance starting in the 1960s, and was a public company from 1965 to 2008. In April 2008, The Midland Company completed a merger with Munich Re, an international insurance

*(Continued)*

business based in Munich, Germany. Ranked 73rd on Fortune Magazine's 2010 Global 500 list, it is one of the world's largest companies. The Midland Company delivers specialized insurance products and services for items such as mobile homes, personal watercraft, classic cars, motorcycles, and snowmobiles.

As a maturing and growing business, the Midland Company found it was using multiple approaches to improve performance and to achieve a sustainable competitive advantage in its chosen markets. While leaders often understood the science of such methodologies and tools, they often did not understand the art of implementation. In the context of the Midland story, methodologies include strategic planning, total quality management, project management, and system development life cycles.

**The key questions Midland leaders faced** are how do these systems and methodologies fit into their overall strategy and how does this help them execute key initiatives? This is the classic three-voice question and the subject of this chapter.

## The Two Dominant Quality Approaches

Quality is one of the few areas that has well established and recognized global standards.

Both of the dominant approaches we cover can be considered standards. As discussed in chapter 1, the use of standards helps to create a common vocabulary and approach that can leverage the talent of your entire organization by focusing on using the standard approaches to improve business results instead of spending time trying to invent a unique methodology for your organization.

This chapter shares the essential concepts and techniques of these dominant quality management methods. Then, these frameworks are systemically used to improve the portfolio and project management methods and culture of your organization. We also describe how several of the more useful additional approaches provide guidance in understanding how customers, employees, and processes interact. Knowledge of these touch points then helps us decide which parts of our existing organization to improve and what new work we need to add to our portfolio.

Table 5.1 summarizes the two dominant quality approaches of Malcolm Baldrige and ISO with the demands each places on CPOs and other executives who are leading work portfolios and project managers.

One concept common to all quality frameworks is that leadership from the top is required to set the tone and create tangible examples for the organization to follow. The variety of leadership responsibilities

*Table 5.1. Combined ISO and Baldrige Principles and Leadership Responsibilities*[1]

| Level | Principles | Leadership responsibilities |
|---|---|---|
| Strategic | Strategic leadership | Establish and communicate vision and values |
| | | Develop and lead implementation of strategy |
| | | Provide necessary resources for implementation |
| Tactical | Customers and other stakeholders | First seek to understand all stakeholders |
| | | Develop relationships with all stakeholders |
| | | Ensure stakeholder satisfaction |
| | Employees | Ensure employees are empowered |
| | | Ensure employees are engaged |
| | | Ensure employees are developing and working together |
| | Processes | Describe and measure processes |
| | | Analyze and understand processes |
| | | Improve processes |
| Both strategic and tactical | Data-based decisions | Gather accurate and reliable customer, employee, and process data |
| | | Use data to understand interdependencies and integrate them |
| | | Make decisions based on factual analysis, judgment, and intuition |

covered in this book start in chapter 2 with identifying, selecting, prioritizing, resourcing, and controlling a portfolio of projects that will best help the organization achieve its strategy and vision subject to constraints. The entire work portfolio process needs to be guided by the leadership team setting and communicating organizational goals and by input from customer voices so that the best set of projects and other work can be selected.

Many of the leadership demands are also included in chapters 3 and 4 with what executives need to do when they serve as a sponsor for a project or have a project manager as a direct report. Data-based decision-making is covered in chapters 6 and 7. We cover the three leadership responsibilities of dealing with customers, employees, and processes in this chapter.

## Customers and Other Stakeholders

Customers are individuals or groups who will use the outputs of a process. They can be internal (within) the producing organization or external to it. External customers are the traditional definition of customers—people who buy your products and/or services. They are the ultimate judge of the quality of your products and services. Internal customers are your employees and suppliers who play a role in the work processes you employ to make and deliver your products and services. When you see work as a process, internal customers are the people who receive the output of the work tasks that precede them. By focusing on both types of customers, you are developing an organization culture that first understands what customer expectations are and then sets about meeting or exceeding these expectations on a consistent basis.

Stakeholders are persons or organizations that are actively involved in the project, whose interests may be positively or negatively impacted by the project, or may exert influence over the project and its deliverables.[2] First you seek to understand who your stakeholders are and then work with them to achieve the best possible outcome that considers their interests.

Customers and other stakeholders today sometimes seem more powerful than ever since they can learn about us and freely share their opinions through the Internet and social media. If we displease a customer, they can let the entire world know about it quickly and in an emotional manner. It has always been important to listen to our customers, but in some ways it is more critical now.

## Understanding Customers and Other Stakeholders

The voice of the customer is the stated and unstated customer needs or requirements.[3] One primary reason we listen to customers and other stakeholders is to obtain actionable information. This information can be used to satisfy their wants and needs, but it can also be to help identify and select potential projects to improve our organizations. While it is widely understood that customer input is important, all too often customer research tells us one thing, but then the customers behave in a different manner. The key is to obtain customer information that accurately predicts their future behavior.

One way to gain customer information is during normal interactions with them. When you provide products and services, make sure you obtain customer feedback as quickly as possible. This can be informal. When seeking customer input more formally through surveys, consider asking questions related to the following five areas:

1. Overall relationship (your importance to them, their satisfaction and loyalty to you),
2. Touch points (where your employees and processes impact customers),
3. Drivers (where you're doing well or poorly has a large impact on them),
4. Ad hoc (changing customer preferences and current strategic needs), and
5. Latent requirements (things you can offer that the customer never considered).[4]

## Developing Relationships with All Stakeholders

Relationships with customers can range from superficial to quite intense. The depth and quality of customer relationships can be expressed at four levels:

1. Confidence—trust in the company and knowing they will always deliver on their promise,
2. Integrity—fair treatment and fair problem resolution,

3. Pride—pride in being a customer and feeling of respect, and

4. Passion—the company is perfect and the world would be less without it.[5]

As you begin to develop a relationship with a customer, you need to start at the first level—demonstrating to that customer that they can have confidence in you. As you satisfy one level in the relationship, you can move to higher levels. There is no substitute for attention and hard work when it comes to developing excellent relationships with customers.

Careful supplier selection makes life easier in many ways. A supplier that can already produce consistently what we need will help us immediately. A supplier that is willing to invest in improvements and learn with us will help us to continually improve. Great suppliers offer improvement suggestions we can use.

### Ensuring Stakeholder Satisfaction

We need to ensure stakeholder satisfaction both at the project level and company level. We have discussed project level satisfaction in chapters 3 and 4. Here we discuss company level satisfaction.

Most successful companies have many stakeholders and a challenge is to treat them all well. At the company level, one needs to develop a sense of balance by not treating one group especially well at the expense of another group. It may be tempting to treat paying customers very well, but causing difficulties for other groups in the process. While this may yield short-term business results, it is often counterproductive toward building sustainable capacity. At the project level, sponsors often determine which stakeholders are relatively more important. That still does not give an excuse to completely ignore less important stakeholders.

When we treat our stakeholders (customers, employees, suppliers, and community) well, many of them develop a sense of ownership in our company. That does not mean they receive monetary profits as our stockholders do, but it means they have a firm desire for us to succeed and they feel they benefit when we succeed. One way to envision this sort of ownership is to consider some of the benefits the United Nations attributes to cooperatives in which stakeholders actually own the organization:

- Cooperatives are open to all persons able to use their services and willing to accept the responsibilities of membership,
- Members actively participate in setting their policies and making decisions, and
- Cooperatives provide education and training for their managers and employees so they can contribute effectively.[6]

We are not suggesting for-profit companies turn themselves into cooperatives, but we are suggesting that by adopting some of the spirit of a cooperative, a for-profit company can enhance the relationships they have with their stakeholders and create both better business results and improved capability.

### Acting upon Customer Voices and Relationships

Once we have heard the customer's voice, we need to describe it in a requirements statement. That is, considering the customer's environment, what is the functional or performance requirement to fulfill the stated need? The customer's requirement will often dictate both enhancements needed in the competencies of our employees and in the capabilities of our processes. Thus, customers, employees, and processes are intertwined and the gaps identified by studying them identify potential projects. In the remainder of this chapter we discuss employee and process voices and in the next chapter we discuss project selection.

# Employees

When understanding and acting appropriately upon the voice of employees, leaders use empowerment, engagement, and teamwork.

### Employee Empowerment

Employee empowerment is trusting in, investing in, and inspiring employees; recognizing their accomplishments, and decentralizing decision-making.[7] Empowerment has sometimes not been understood well.

To truly empower an employee, she needs to be given enough information, training, and confidence to progressively make more important decisions. Employee empowerment is a process, not an event. As an employee develops the judgment and confidence to make more decisions, the supervisor is freed to spend more time on higher level issues. Thus both the employee and the supervisor benefit.

### Employee Engagement

Employee engagement occurs when workers are emotionally and psychologically committed to the organization, feel a strong sense of ownership in the organization's success, and want to contribute to its improved performance.[8] Great organizations recognize that their employees are an exceptional asset. The employees are encouraged to provide ideas on how their work should be improved and are given the freedom and resources (within reason) to recommend and act on ideas that can help meet or exceed customer expectations.

Another aspect of employee engagement is the investment the organization makes in communicating with and training their people so they have the skills and knowledge they need to solve customer problems effectively. Just as customer relationships can be measured and developed at four levels, so can employee engagement, by having each employee progressively answer these sets of questions:

1. Do I know what is expected of me and do I have the equipment I need?
2. Do I get to do what I do best, do I get recognized, and does someone care about me and help me develop?
3. Does my opinion count, do I feel aligned with the company mission, do my coworkers want to improve, and do I have a best friend at work?
4. Is someone measuring my progress and giving me opportunities to grow?[9]

### Employee Development and Teamwork

There are many aspects to employee development. In portfolio and project management, perhaps the most important is teamwork. Teamwork occurs in a workgroup that possesses a clear mission, effective leadership, shared values and behavior norms, trust, openness, and commitment.[10] Teamwork means that cross-functional teams are commonplace to solve far-reaching company problems and work on new ideas from multiple functional perspectives. Teamwork also extends beyond the four walls of your own organization to include your key suppliers, customers, as well as other stakeholder organizations such as labor unions and educational institutions. Working with an end-to-end perspective with many parties actively involved provides better and more holistic solutions to challenging opportunities.

# Process

A process is usually thought of as a series of activities executed and decisions made to perform specific tasks, such as paying a bill, shipping a product, and even more complex processes like that of developing a new product or service.

### Describe and Measure Processes

When studying a process, in addition to the activities performed and decisions made, people often also consider the inputs that are needed and who supplies each at the front end and the outputs created and who the customers of each are at the back end as shown in Figure 5.1. By seeing work as a process, one is able to analyze how things are done now and, through objective data, identify where improvements are needed. Another reason seeing work as a process is so effective is that many work

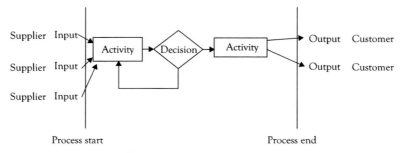

*Figure 5.1. Process illustration.*

processes today in organizations cross many parts of the organization and are cross-functional. By analyzing cross-functional work processes (versus analyzing by function) you are examining your organization much more holistically and developing insights at a deeper level.

### Analyze and Understand Processes

The voice of the process is the data describing actual performance that can be used to predict the future average and natural process limits that define the range of outputs that can be expected from a process.[11] We gather data concerning the inputs, activities, and outputs of our processes so we can understand, control, and improve them. If we continue to perform our processes in the current manner, we can expect the same range of results. Thus, the range of current results predicts the expected range of future results, unless we make changes. These current process results along with our knowledge of how the process currently operates is the voice of the process. We need this understanding as a starting point for controlling and improving the process. Controlling a process means monitoring it to ensure we continue to receive the predicted range of outputs that it is normally capable of producing. If that normal range fully satisfies all of our customers, we might be content with how that particular process is performing. However, in most companies, some processes are in need of improvement at any point in time.

### Improve Processes

Process improvement includes both incremental and large, break-through changes to a process to enhance customer value, reduce problems, increase productivity, and/or improve responsiveness.[12] Process improvement is sometimes called continuous improvement. The term continuous improvement can be challenging because it implies you are never done! Based on your knowledge of your customer's dynamically changing needs, you will need to be finding ways to improve your work processes to meet your customer's evolving needs. The changes you make can be small, incremental, and gradual changes or breakthrough, large, and rapid changes that result in significant improvements. Most companies have both small and large changes most of the time. Deciding which processes need change the most is a prioritization decision covered in chapter 2.

Process Improvement Approaches

One common approach advocated today is **Six Sigma**. Six Sigma has two meanings. The literal meaning is you want your quality to be so good, that the variation in your process results from the average to the customer's tolerance limit is six standard deviations. That literally means you would have no more than a handful of items out of every million that were not good enough for the customer! Even many people who are strong advocates of Six Sigma will tell you candidly that achieving true Six Sigma results on all of their processes all of the time is an aspirational goal—not easily achieved. The second meaning of Six Sigma is a dedication to continuous improvement in an effort to improve process performance in the direction of Six Sigma or near perfection.

Six Sigma has multiple themes, just as ISO and Baldrige do. In practice, the larger focus is often on process improvement—and especially on reducing cost and time in work processes. Six Sigma major themes can be envisioned as:

- Fact-driven management with top down metrics and rigorous statistical analysis,
- Process understanding, control, and improvement particularly to save time and money,
- Goal setting to objectively select improvement projects and set stretch goals,
- Define project sponsors and experts (black belts) and to collaborate during each project, and
- Use the define, measure, analyze, improve and control (DMAIC) process to guide the projects.

**Lean** is another management approach designed to reduce cost, reduce time, and improve quality in work processes. A lean approach accomplishes this by eliminating all forms of waste and creating smooth flows of materials and information.[13] Lean uses simple tools to identify and remove from a process anything that does not add value. It promotes sustainability as less energy and fewer materials are wasted. Lean and Six Sigma are often used together. The simple approaches of Lean can be used quickly by most people, but the more statistical tools of Six Sigma are best led by a highly trained person.

**Business process re-engineering (BPR)** is the fundamental analysis and, frequently the radical redesign of how work is performed. The basic question BPR answers is not how can we make a process more efficient, but do we even need this process? The primary goal of BPR is similar to that of both Six Sigma and Lean—namely to reduce the cost and time it takes to produce the goods and services needed for our customers. However, while Six Sigma uses statistical analysis and Lean uses simple tools, BPR starts with a clean page and asks, if we could design this process from scratch, what would it look like?

All three of these approaches often work together. Rather than worry about which approach is best, let us focus on a process improvement methodology.

Process Improvement Methodology

How do you go about analyzing your work processes to make changes? The literature is full of process improvement methods. We show the two most common types of models. Figure 5.2 is a plan, do, study, act (PDCA) model. People who use Six Sigma as their quality improvement guide, use the DMAIC model to guide their improvements. Figure 5.3 is a DMAIC model. Both PDCA and DMAIC models are very similar and both are widely used.

Any good improvement model is based on the scientific process. That is, one starts with a hypothesis—an educated guess. That implies both knowledge of how the current process works and supporting data. The next step in the scientific process is to try an experiment while collecting data. The results of the experiment are compared with the previous results to determine any impact. Finally, if the results look promising, the experiment is often conducted multiple times under varying circumstances before confirming a theory. Likewise, with improvement models, a pilot

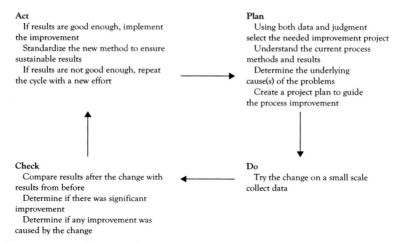

**Act**
If results are good enough, implement the improvement
Standardize the new method to ensure sustainable results
If results are not good enough, repeat the cycle with a new effort

**Plan**
Using both data and judgment select the needed improvement project
Understand the current process methods and results
Determine the underlying cause(s) of the problems
Create a project plan to guide the process improvement

**Check**
Compare results after the change with results from before
Determine if there was significant improvement
Determine if any improvement was caused by the change

**Do**
Try the change on a small scale collect data

*Figure 5.2. Plan Do Check Act (PDCA) Model.*[14]

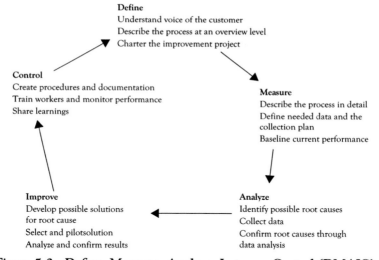

**Define**
Understand voice of the customer
Describe the process at an overview level
Charter the improvement project

**Control**
Create procedures and documentation
Train workers and monitor performance
Share learnings

**Measure**
Describe the process in detail
Define needed data and the collection plan
Baseline current performance

**Improve**
Develop possible solutions for root cause
Select and pilotsolution
Analyze and confirm results

**Analyze**
Identify possible root causes
Collect data
Confirm root causes through data analysis

*Figure 5.3. Define, Measure, Analyze, Improve, Control (DMAIC) Model.*

is often repeated and expanded prior to instituting an organization-wide implementation with full controls.

Any good improvement model is also based upon solid project management practice. The first step is to select the project that will be most useful based upon both the needs of the company and its customers. Then develop a high-level overall understanding of the customer needs, current process, the team who will perform the improvement, and overall plan. This is normally agreed to in the form of a charter to quickly ensure everyone understands and commits. Then more detailed planning and early implementing take place—often on an iterative basis to ensure the approach works. The remaining implementation is completed. The customer confirms that the resulting deliverables suit their needs. The implementation team transitions the deliverables to the users along with any help they may need to be successful. The implementation team also feeds lessons learned back into the system to improve future projects. Finally, after the customer has used the project for some time, a further analysis is completed to verify the promised benefits are being delivered.

Process Improvement Teams

A process improvement team is usually chartered and empowered by the management of the organization. The charter, as described in chapter 2, may specify which process they want improved and why. The charter should specify your problem boundaries, and any constraints you have as you go after this problem. If you have not been "given" a problem/process to solve, then you will need to select what problem to go after. A simple but effective way to do this is to get input on key processes that people in your organization and your customers believe could be and need to be improved and then evaluate these problems using criteria such as:

- How important is this process to your customers? (1–10 scale)
- Do you believe you have the skills and resources to improve this process? (1–10 scale)
- How difficult will it be to improve this process? (1–10 scale)

Once you have picked the problem/process to improve, you may want to modify or select the team who will work on this based on their skills and knowledge of this process area.

When you analyze the current situation, use analytical tools to flow chart the process(es) and gather quantitative measures to describe what is going on in the process as well as describing the end results of the process(es). These two types of measures are called in-process measures and outcome measures. In-process measures help you see the process activity such as how many transactions are flowing, how long in time it takes for each step in the process, etc. Outcome measures quantify the final results such as the total costs of this transaction, and final quality measures relevant to this process.

The remaining steps in this process improvement method are focused on identifying and verifying root causes or cause and effect relationships that will help you put in place solutions that can improve your processes. This will be all about the quality of your data and how well you can analyze that data to understand where your improvement opportunities are. Once you find a solution that demonstrates that it can work, you standardize by documenting the new process and train your people in this new and improved process. You then move on to find your next improvement opportunity.

## Combining Customers, Employees, and Processes

A key aspect of making your company's strategy comes to life is the selecting and implementing of strategic projects that will deliver the best short- and long-term business results. Customer satisfaction, employee development, and process improvement needs can be used in selecting the best work portfolio. Once you select a project to implement, you need to execute with excellence by using proven project management principles to achieve an on-time and on-budget execution that delivers the promised business benefits.

Portfolio Management is used to link your organization's strategy to specific projects. The best portfolio decisions are made based upon key quantitative measures that are meaningful to your key customers.

Individual projects are better when using a customer-focused approach to ensure desired results are delivered. Many projects are undertaken to significantly improve existing work processes. Projects are guided by objective in-process and outcome measures.

Improving your organization's culture and operating methods takes a concerted effort. This use of these principles to lead the organization needs to be driven both top-down and bottom-up. Top-down implementation needs to come from making clear strategic choices and communicating them by explaining why these strategies were chosen. Leadership can demonstrate their commitment to quality by setting measurable goals for each strategy and holding quarterly reviews to assess progress. Those in leadership roles can examine their own work processes. Chartering process improvement teams will also empower people to apply these quality principles where they live and work each day.

Bottom-up change can be seen when people at each level in the organization focus on the customer of their work and make changes to delight those customers. Making decisions based on well-defined and objective data is another way people can live by these quality principles. Employees can form process improvement teams that focus on the most important and impactful work processes. This will make significant and lasting changes and provide momentum to the widespread and successful use of these quality approaches.

Specifically, a CPO can do several things to build the project culture. She can insist that all project managers stay close to their customers. She can ensure all projects have signed charters to guarantee they are initiated well. She can insist on adequate project documentation so decisions are made based upon facts. She can develop a project management community of practice within the company to promote continual improvement of project processes. She can join an external community of practice for executives. She can develop and oversee a project career path so project managers who aspire to become executives understand what they need to learn and demonstrate. She can work with executives and managers throughout the company to ensure they understand what a good project culture looks like.

## Midland Case to Improve Performance

Initially, leaders at Midland understood the value of performance improvement techniques and quality management (science), but what they also learned over time was the art that would take the business to the next level. The next level was not just listening to and understanding the voices of customers, employees, and process. It was also understanding the linkages between the voices in regards to

*(Continued)*

(*Continued*)

strategy and, more importantly, the execution of strategy and business improvement.

Midland's focus is superior execution of strategy. Superior execution is brought back to three main core processes (voices) of execution.

- Strategy Process—Making the link with Operations and Employees
  - Customer is the primary building block
- Employee Process—Making the link with Strategy and Operations
- Operations Process—Making the link with Strategy and Employee.

The Project Office Exhibit (Figure 5.4) illustrates a framework of how strategy, operations, and business improvement were integrated together in the day-to-day business.

### Lessons Learned

Art versus Science

This chapter discusses the importance of building a foundation of performance improvement around three main building blocks (Customer, Employee, and Process). While conceptually deploying various approaches and tools to operationalize improvement makes all the sense in the world, implementation can be tricky. At the Midland Company, through trial and error, navigation for our leaders and associates became an obstacle to implementation. Until Midland executives achieved a common understanding of how the different approaches and tools fit into our business, implementation, and impact was minimal. The Project Office Exhibit illustrates the framework we created to help build this common understanding in the organization. This framework assisted people in understanding how improvement fits into our business system. It also helped reduce complexity. Most importantly, it helped people "connect the dots" on the cause and effect of operational improvement, project work, and ultimately overall strategy. As your organization grapples with achieving current business success while improving capability, helping them

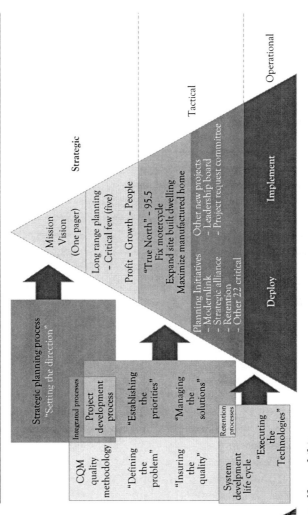

*Figure 5.4. Project office exhibit.*

understand what approaches work for strategy and what approaches work for day-to-day improvement is essential.

Establishing a navigational framework was also beneficial for our leaders. It provided a framework for assessing, prioritizing, and packaging projects and new initiatives. The framework helped them understand how a new business improvement methodology fits into our business system, and helped on-board new employees as they joined the organization.

## Common Language

Related to establishing a common framework for improvement in the organization was creation of a common language. Assuming listening points for customer, employee, and process are established, creation of a common language will remove the mystery and confusion for the organization. In Midland's improvement journey, we often asked the organization to "work smarter" and "listen to the customer," but we found without the common approach or a common language, the meaning was often lost in translation. As Midland matured in quality, terms such as *voice of the customer* and *process improvement* were universally understood and the organization could mobilize process improvement teams and initiatives much quicker.

## Process Ownership

Another obstacle encountered on Midland's improvement journey was the concept of Process Ownership. Operationalizing quality concepts, action plans, and improvement teams can be difficult without clear process ownership across an operation's core process families. For example, Midland's product development process had four functions that were accountable for certain aspects of this core insurance process. The four functions involved, owned, and optimized their part of the process, but no one owned all of it. This created frustration when mobilizing quality and process improvement approaches and teams.

Several solutions were deployed to optimize performance improvement in this example. To facilitate process ownership, organizational design and structure changes were made. This reduced fragmentation and built broader process ownership. While structural change was an

(Continued)

important tool in solving process ownership issues, several other techniques were used to facilitate process improvement. Common process **scorecards** were shared across process participants who jointly developed process metrics and goals around cost, quality, and service. As joint process metrics were integrated across process participants, the roll-out of **master schedule** and resource plan was developed as a by-product of these discussions. As process owners discussed joint goals, the optimization and proper use of resources were jointly planned across functions.

Marty Novakov,

*Vice President, Strategy Management,*

*American Modern Insurance Group, Munich Re America*

# How Listening to Customers, Employees, and Processes Can Help Achieve Competing Objectives

### *Executives Setting Strategy and Managers Implementing It*

Executives and managers can use customer, employee, and process voices and their interactions to set strategy and operate effectively. They can request input from the rank and file employees as strategies are being established. Both executives and managers can use clear goals and measures to establish quantitative targets that clarify what success looks like. Operational people can assess if the project plans are sufficient to hit the strategies goals.

### *Sustainable Organizational Capability and Current Business Results*

Quality is a "both/and" approach where you can have high quality and low costs. By effectively leading the interactions with customers, employees, and processes you can create good short-term business results and build organizational capability at the same time. By focusing on your customer and delighting them with your products and services you can achieve good current business results. When utilizing process improvement techniques, employees are also increasing long-term capability. For example, when developing customer complaint systems, make sure appropriate feedback goes to the applicable department.

### Project Goals and Operational Goals

When projects apply data-based decision-making, projects have a much better chance of reaching their successful milestones or being clear on why they will not be able to be successful. This transparency will assist project managers in making good decisions based on the facts. Employees can apply the same principle in day-to-day operations. Daily management measures of process results can be used to monitor if a process is within stable control or has enough variability to be classified as out of control and needing corrective action. Having such an effective daily management system in place helps operations reach predictable and successful results.

### One Function's Goals and Another Function's Goals

Because quality approaches allow you to examine and improve work processes that cross-functional boundaries as well as those processes within an individual function, quality can be applied both within a function and to an entire organization. Therefore quality principles enable you to achieve results in the targeted functions of your work or the entire set of functions present in your organization. The principles that are most helpful for functional work are data-based decision making, process management, and customer-centric focus.

## Top 10 Assessment Questions

1. Describe the core quality principles exhibited in your company.
2. Describe how these principles shape some of your daily (or at least frequent) actions and interactions with others.
3. Describe how your personal core quality principles shape your organization's leadership approach to portfolio and project management.

4. What does your organization specifically do to understand the expectations of your external and internal customers?

5. How do you engage both your employees and suppliers to work collaboratively to meet the expectations of your external and internal customers?

6. Can you and everyone else in your organization illustrate how a few key work activities form a process with inputs, activities, decisions, and outputs?

7. Describe how people in your organization work individually to improve their specific work and collaboratively to improve cross-functional work.

8. What process improvement methodology do you use?

9. Do you formally charter process improvement teams?

10. How do process improvement goals get set how is progress toward them reported?

# APPENDIX A

# Two Dominant Quality Standards

## Malcolm Baldrige National Quality Award

Table 5A.1 shows the primary criteria used in assessing and awarding the Malcolm Baldrige National Quality award for TQM. This is a very prestigious award and is viewed as a key accomplishment by any organization that wins this award. It is an award developed in the United States.

*Table 5A.1. Malcolm Baldrige Performance Excellence Principles and Leadership Responsibilities*[15]

| Level | Principles | Leadership responsibilities |
|---|---|---|
| Strategic | Leadership | Set and deploy vision and values |
| | | Create sustainable organization through learning |
| | | Accomplish objectives and improve performance through action |
| | Strategic planning | Develop strategy to address short and long time horizons |
| | | Develop and deploy action plans to achieve strategic objectives |
| | | Ensure resources to accomplish action plans and meet current obligations |
| Tactical | Customer focus | Listen to voice of customer to obtain actionable information |
| | | Determine customer satisfaction and engagement |
| | | Build and manage customer relationships |
| | Workforce focus | Assess and improve your workforce capability, capacity, and engagement |

*(Continued)*

*Table 5A.1. Malcolm Baldrige Performance Excellence Principles and Leadership Responsibilities[15]—(Continued)*

| Level | Principles | Leadership responsibilities |
|---|---|---|
| | | Manage your workforce to accomplish organization's work |
| | | Use a learning system to meet both short-term and long-term goals |
| | Operations focus | Design and innovate your work processes to meet all key requirements |
| | | Manage your supply chain for performance and customer satisfaction |
| | | Improve your work processes |
| Both strategic and tactical | Measurement, analysis, and knowledge | Use voice of customer to support strategic decision making |
| | | Use daily operations and performance improvement measures |
| | | Collect and transfer customer and workforce knowledge |
| | Results | Levels and trends in process performance measures |
| | | Levels and trends in customer satisfaction |
| | | Levels and trends in workforce capability, capacity, and development |
| | | Levels and trends in financial and marketplace performance |

# ISO 9001:2008

The ISO 9000 family of standards, developed in Europe by the International Organization for Standardization, represents an international consensus on good quality management practices. It consists of standards and guidelines relating to quality management systems and related supporting standards. ISO 9001:2008 is the set of standardized requirements for a quality management system, regardless of what the user organization does, its size, or whether it is in the private, or public sector.

This standard provides a tried and tested framework for taking a systematic approach to managing the organization's processes so that they consistently turn out product that satisfies customers' expectations.

ISO 9001:2008 lays down what requirements your quality system must meet, but does not dictate how they should be met in any particular organization. This leaves great scope and flexibility for implementation in different business sectors and business cultures, as well as in different national cultures.[16] Table 5A.2 presents the current principles embodied by ISO 9000:2008.

*Table 5A.2. ISO 9001 Quality Principles and Leadership Responsibilities*[17]

| Level | Principle | Leadership responsibilities |
|---|---|---|
| Strategic | Leadership | Establish and communicate a clear vision of the organization's future |
| | | Create and sustain shared values at all levels of the organization |
| | | Provide people with the needed resources, training, and freedom to act |
| | Systems approach | Understand the interdependencies between key processes |
| | | Reduce cross-functional barriers |
| | | Continually improve the system through measurement and evaluation |
| | Mutually beneficial | Identify and select key suppliers carefully |
| | Supplier | Establish relationships that balance short term and long term |
| | Relationships | Establish joint development and improvement activities |
| Tactical | Customer Focus | Link organizational objectives to customer needs and expectations |
| | | Measure customer satisfaction and results |
| | | Manage customer relationships |

(*Continued*)

*Table 5A.2. IS0 9001 Quality Principles and Leadership Responsibilities[17]—(Continued)*

| Level | Principle | Leadership responsibilities |
|---|---|---|
| | Involvement of people | Ensure people understand their importance in the organization |
| | | Encourage people to seek opportunities to enhance their competence |
| | | Establish a culture where people will freely discuss problems |
| | Process approach | Systematically define processes needed to obtain desired results |
| | | Identify process interfaces between organization and customers |
| | | Measure, analyze, and improve key processes |
| Both strategic and tactical | Continual improvement | Employ a consistent approach to continual improvement |
| | | Establish goals to guide, and measures to track, improvement |
| | | Recognize and acknowledge improvements |
| | Factual approach to decision-making | Make decisions and take action based upon factual analysis, balanced with experience and intuition |
| | | Ensure that data and information are accurate and reliable |
| | | Make data and information available to those who need it |

# CHAPTER 6

# Understanding Information Technology Opportunities and Challenges: A Chief Information Officer's Role

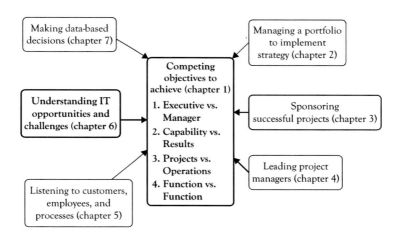

For many organizations, information technology (IT) can be a confusing, intimidating, and costly area. The technical jargon, endless acronyms, and IT professionals who speak "geek" and not in business terms can be very frustrating. The executive role clearly most impacted by information technology is that of chief information officer (CIO) or the senior IT manager who leads the use of IT for the organization. The CIO role or senior IT manager has evolved significantly over the last several years. This role today needs to deliver functional/technical excellence and also be business driven to make sure that IT investments enable the organization's business strategy.

The purpose of this chapter is to:

- Equip you with the basics of information technology,
- Acquaint you with what is possible using this technology,
- Enable you to develop a strategic IT master plan for your organization,
- Outline practical advice on how and when to use IT consultants, and
- Give you insight on how best to select and work with software vendors.

Becoming competent in information technology will help organizations bridge the gap between strategy and execution.

Literally every organization today depends on information technology to operate. It is imperative that your organization develop and execute an IT strategy and overall master plan that enables you to be successful with your overall business strategy.

IT is used in so many areas to automate business processes that it is very easy to get distracted with supporting and improving your existing IT systems, when in fact, the strategic question of where should we focus our IT resources for competitive advantage is the key task requiring our portfolio decisions.

As you look to execute projects of all types in your organization to implement change, most of these projects will have significant IT components and application systems directly involved.

Information technology can be leveraged to significantly change your business model to compete in today's markets. IT is a strategic component for radical change. In Thomas Friedman's groundbreaking book, The World is Flat,[1] he explains how 10 key forces are at work to make the world a level playing field for people in all countries around the world. Eight of the ten forces have either a direct (e.g., #9 = In-Forming—Google, Yahoo, and MSN Web Search) or an applied use (#7 = Supply Chaining) of IT.

It is for these reasons that we have chosen to include a chapter on information technology.

This chapter provides a basic framework to help you understand what IT is all about. If you do not have a working knowledge of the basics of

IT, we have provided appendices that explain the basics of the major areas of IT (e.g., hardware, software, networks, the Internet).

For people who have a working knowledge of IT, the chapter starts at the level of significant new developments in IT that are relevant for today's organizations. We cover applied topics that someone leading an organization will need to think about, such as how to design your future enterprise IT architecture and corresponding master plan. Having an IT master plan will enable you to align your IT investments to achieve your organization's strategic goals. This is a specific example of portfolio management covered in chapter 3.

## YourEncore Case to Select Critical Packaged Software

A common and very strategic task that many small-to medium-sized organizations have to do is select a vendor-supplied software package to run a major part of their organization.

YourEncore is a privately held company established in 2003 by founding Member Companies, The Procter & Gamble Company, Eli Lilly and Company, and The Boeing Company. YourEncore is a company of veteran scientific, engineering, and technical experts that provides clients with solutions based on a lifetime of proven expertise. YourEncore deploys its expertise against capability, capacity, and technical challenges in a confidential environment to help clients develop products essential to healthier, safer, and richer lives.

YourEncore had to replace a set of home-grown systems they used to run their financial transactions as well as manage ongoing projects. We share in this chapter an example of how YourEncore identified, evaluated, selected, and implemented a commercial vendor package to fit the needs of the company.

**The key questions YourEncore leaders** faced were first, "Are our IT systems strong enough to support their future?" Then second, "Should we staff our own IT organization to build our own solution or should we buy the best commercial software to meet our needs?" These are examples of questions asking whether information technology is a strategic weapon for your organization and industry or whether it is a tactical necessity.

## Information Technology—A Basic Framework

To help keep it simple, the major categories of information technology that we include in the basic framework are software, hardware, telecommunications, and database technology.[2]

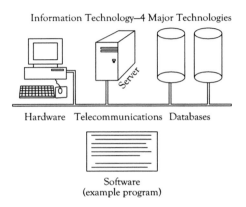

Information Technology—4 Major Technologies

Hardware    Telecommunications    Databases

Software
(example program)

## Software (See Appendix B for the Basics of Software)

### Software As A Service (SaaS)

A recent innovation that enables organizations to use software on an as-needed basis without expensive software licenses is software as a service (SaaS).

An important tactical decision that you will need to make is whether your organization will own (lease or buy) its own computer hardware and software, or whether you will buy services from a company that provides "software as a service." In the SaaS scenario, the company providing the service owns the hardware and relevant software licenses and provides you the ability to interact with their hardware and software to use the application software you need when you need it. An early example of a SaaS offering that is broadly used is a customer relationship management (CRM) application called SALESFORCE.COM.[3,4]

# Hardware (See Appendix B for the Basics of Hardware)

The term hardware refers to the physical equipment that the software runs on. Most people really don't need to know too much about computer hardware. It's like owning a car—how much do you need to know about the details of the engine versus how to drive and maintain the car?

Hardware can range from small personal digital assistants (PDAs), to personal computers, to midrange computers or servers, to large mainframe computers, all the way up to supercomputers. As computers get larger they typically get faster and have more storage capacity to run more software and store more data.

# Telecommunications (See Appendix B for the Basics of Telecommunications)

One of the key characteristics of using computers today is the ability to communicate and transfer data across physical locations, especially for people who work in organizations that have several locations across the world. Whether you are sending an email message, are tweeting with someone, or interacting with one of your customers or suppliers such as invoicing or sharing inventory data, the ability to share information and data of all sorts across physical locations is a critical aspect of using computer technology. Telecommunications is a term that refers to communicating between devices on common carrier networks. Sometimes people also call this area of technology computer networks.

# The Internet (See Appendix B for Basics on Internet)

Clearly one of the biggest and most impactful uses of computer technology has been the advent of the Internet—often called the World Wide Web or the Net. It is a network of networks. In fact the name Internet is short for the term internetwork. The Internet is basically the ability of computer networks of all types (private, public, universities, business, government, etc.) around the world to connect by all using the same transmission protocol (TCP/IP—discussed later). This creates a global network of almost unlimited capacity and scope.

## Database Management Technology (See Appendix B for Basics on Databases)

Databases, as the name implies, are the electronic storage of very large collections of data. Data is a critical asset for most organizations and organizing and storing this key information is an important capability of computer technology.

## Queries, Business Intelligence, and Data Visualization

One of the most important things to do with data held in databases is to access it, produce meaningful reports, and to analyze the data using a range of sophisticated analytical tools. There is a broad spectrum of ways to access and look at data. The umbrella term of business intelligence (BI) is being used to denote many different ways of "examining the interrelationships of presented facts in such a way as to guide actions toward a desired goal."[5] BI is one of the fastest areas of innovation and new developments.

The spectrum of BI tools include the following major types:

1. Dashboard—The ability to publish a formal report online with intuitive visual display of information including dials, gauges, and traffic lights indicating the state of performance.[6]
2. Drillable Data—The ability to click on data presented on the screen, with the resulting display being the underlying data—that is, drilling down a level of detail.
3. Standard Reporting—Provide preformatted, "canned" reports whose measure and dimension types are predefined, where user parameters can optionally be provided to select the specific rows for their business need.
4. Save As Excel—Microsoft Excel is such a dominantly used tool that any list of BI tools must include Excel, either as a tool used directly with the data, or as a common medium for exchange/transport.

5. Ad Hoc—End-users being able to generate new or modified queries with significant flexibility over content, layout, and calculations.
6. Analytics—Application of statistical methods against select data to solve specific questions.
7. Advanced Visualization—The ability to display numerous aspects of the data more efficiently by using interactive pictures and charts instead of rows and columns.
8. Off-line—Off-line capabilities imply that even though the user is disconnected from the network, they can still access the data they need and perform whatever reporting/analysis functions they require.

## New Business Models Enabled by the Internet

The classic justification of using computer technology in businesses was to automate transactions (e.g., order management, accounts receivables, etc.) to reduce the amount of people needed to perform these tasks, improve speed, and overall efficiency and accuracy, and primarily to reduce costs. This cost savings business model is still evident in business today, but with the advent of the Internet and several other improvements in computer technology (e.g., graphical user interfaces, the Internet, much more capable software applications in many areas), computer technology is enabling other business benefits such as faster innovation, deeper insight into data, and the ability to do things virtually versus physically.

As described briefly in the Internet section, the Web has evolved from a static source of information like a newspaper or a library (i.e., Internet 1.0), to a shared canvas where the contributions made by one party can be enhanced and built upon by others (i.e., Internet 2.0). In their book, Wikinomics, How Mass Collaboration Changes Everything, Don Tapscott and Anthony D. Williams explain how business models can be created to leverage this new world of Internet 2.0 in dramatic new ways.[7]

### Open Innovation

Let us first look at the business model of open innovation.[8] Usually, companies have their own research and development (R&D) staffs on their payrolls and they guard their R&D work as critical proprietary information as top secret from the world outside their company walls. Procter & Gamble realized that they could not innovate and create new products fast enough to meet their future financial goals with only the P&G R&D employees on their payroll.[9] The amount of expertise and available new product ideas and ready to roll prototypes that exist around the world and are now accessible via the Web make the concept of open innovation a viable business option.

Open innovation encourages companies to access external ideas as well as their own internal ideas, and to pursue collaboration and partnerships to change how new products and services are developed and brought to market.

A classic case of open innovation is the story of Goldcorp Inc. and how by sharing what was thought to be proprietary data, they were able to access outside innovation expertise and literally save their company. Goldcorp is a Toronto-based gold mining firm that was in deep financial trouble in the late 1990s. They had ceased mining operations because of labor strikes, high debts, and a very high cost of production. Without evidence of significant new gold deposits, Goldcorp looked like it was to shut down.

The CEO, Rob McEwen, gathered his R&D staff of geologists and challenged them to put together a plan to find more gold on their property holdings. Early test drillings were very promising but the geologists could not provide accurate estimates of the location of gold and its value. McEwen had an inspiration while he was attending an MIT seminar where he heard the story of how the Linux computer operating system was created by thousands of volunteer programmers working together under the leadership of a scientist named Linus Torvalds.[10]

McEwen's idea was to share all the geological data Goldcorp had on its property with the world via the Internet and harness the best minds in the world to identify where the next six million ounces of gold could be found on Goldcorp land. He created a contest in March of 2000 with total prize money of $575,000 that would be awarded to participants who were judged to have the best ideas. The results of this contest were amazing:

1. Entries came in from geologists but also from scientists in math, advanced physics, intelligent systems, computer graphics, and organic solutions to inorganic problems.

2. A 110 targets were identified with 50% of these targets not being previously identified. Over 80% of the new targets yielded substantial quantities of gold.

3. Goldcorp went from being an underperforming $100 million company to a $9 billion powerhouse.

There are many other novel business models enabled by leveraging the capabilities of Internet 2.0. The basic principles of this mode of working that Tapscott and Williams term "Wikinomics" are:

- Being open—look externally as well as internally
- Peering—access expertise and share information to do it
- Sharing—rather than controlling, find good opportunities to share ideas
- Acting globally—access expertise from all around the world and in all disciplines.

In summary, Wikinomics enables different business models when individuals and companies use widely distributed computation and communications technologies to achieve shared outcomes through new types of voluntary associations.[11]

## IT Architecture and Master Planning

There is an inherent human need to see how things fit together—especially when confronted with a complex picture of many items. Such is the case when looking at an organization and how it can best use computer technology to meet its business objectives. This section presents a best approach for developing and implementing an information technology enterprise architecture and resulting master plan/action for implementing projects to achieve the defined future state.

An enterprise architecture is like a city plan for your city or town. For a city plan, you need to have a "big picture" vision that transcends individual units (buildings, services) and focuses on the way collections of units (neighborhoods, communities) can fulfill a variety of different purposes. A city planner puts in place the foundation and infrastructure that enable the city to thrive and prosper and be interconnected via a variety of common services (e.g., utilities).[12]

## A City Planning Example

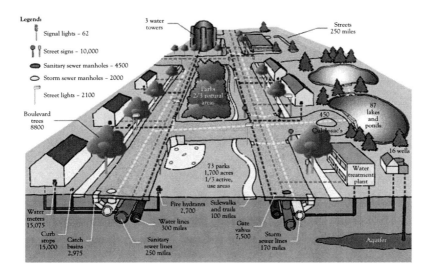

The IT enterprise architecture does the same thing for an organization and how it plans to use and leverage information technology. There are four major areas when considering how best to apply information technology to an organization:

1. Work/business processes
2. Information/data
3. Computer applications
4. Computer infrastructure.

These areas may be fairly obvious. It is interesting to note that the two areas of business processes and data are not always intuitive to business leaders as areas that need to be considered when defining an IT architecture.

The basic approach for defining an IT architecture is to:

- Understand the business strategy in-depth.
- Do an environmental scan to know what is happening in your industry for the next few years and how other firms are intending to deal with these challenges.
- Develop the fundamental architectural principles the organization has chosen to follow.
- Then examine the current state for each of the four areas listed above.
- Define the future state for each of the four areas listed above.

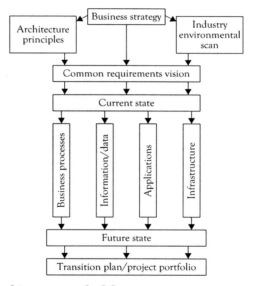

*Enterprise architecture methodology.*
*Source: P&G.*

Two factors must be taken into account when following this methodology. First, not all of these four areas are equally important for all organizations. For example, if a company has adopted and purchased software for their enterprise (e.g., SAP, ORACLE), the application area may already be determined given this software selection. So you need to tailor how much attention you pay to each of the four areas given your business situation.

The second factor that comes into play is the level of detail that you use for the current and future state analysis. For example, if you are looking to improve your applications incrementally, that will require a much lower level of detail analysis than if your industry is undergoing radical change and you need to blow up your current state applications and radically change what you do in the future. This could require a much more detailed future state definition.

Once you have the current state and future state architectures defined, you need to develop a transition plan. This is comprised of projects that when implemented will transform your current state into the future state you have developed to meet your business needs. This transition plan could be one complex project that gets you all the way to the future state (sometimes called a "big bang" approach), or it could be a series of smaller projects that get you to the future state over time. Each project will need to deliver tangible business benefits that pay for the cost of doing each project.

### *"Big Bang" Transition Plan*

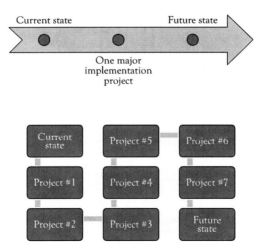

# Transition Plan Requiring Several Steps (Each Project Delivers Tangible Benefits)

You can think of this transition plan as a portfolio of projects leading to the future state you have defined for your organization. These projects will likely have to compete with other projects being considered in your project portfolio management process.

The most difficult aspect of doing transition planning is constructing defined projects that each deliver sufficient business benefits that justify doing the project, but when taken all together get you from your current state to your defined future state. Sometimes you may have to include putting in some key pieces of infrastructure (e.g., additional computer network capacity) into the economics of a project that requires this infrastructure. Justifying infrastructure projects alone without the key applications that require them is often very difficult.

See Appendix C for information on an emerging global standard for a proven methodology to do enterprise IT architectures.

# Dealing with Software Vendors

A basic principle that many organizations have adopted is to buy versus build their own software. This allows you to be a customer of a carefully selected, high-quality vendor versus being in the business of developing and supporting your own software by using resources on your staff. Buying software is typically much less costly (when looking at the total costs) and more effective in giving you software that has new capabilities added to it over time in a timely fashion.

However, it is important to understand some basic facts on how software vendors operate and how best to deal with them. I will deal primarily with application software vendors (versus software vendors who write systems software like operating systems or programming languages, etc.) since that is what most organizations care about the most.

### Selecting Software Packages (See Appendix D for Basics on Commercial Software)

When evaluating potential application software packages it is important to do this well, because once you have made an investment in a software vendor and their products, the cost and time to switch choices is very large and not easy (although it can be done). Typically, people look at a shortlist of market leading vendors for the application area they are most interested in. The factors I suggest people consider are:[13]

- "Have to have" major functionality features—the things the software **must** do.
- "Nice to have"—features that are not required but could be very helpful.
- Does this package comply with the important standards in this application area?
- Total cost of ownership—purchase costs, maintenance costs, training costs, operating costs.
- Strength of vendor factors:

    ○ Is this a thought leading vendor? Will they improve their product regularly?
    ○ Will this vendor be in business for the long term?
    ○ What is this vendor's track record regarding new releases, quality, and stability of their products?
    ○ What do the current customers of this vendor think about this vendor and how they operate?
    ○ Can you work with and trust this vendor?
    ○ Does the vendor operate in all the geographies you need?
    ○ Other factors?

### Software Sales Representatives

As stated before, software sales can be very lucrative and as such are normally staffed by aggressive sales people who are driven to meet customer needs by selling products and services. It is not unusual that these positions turn over often. Therefore, when trying to get accurate information about current or potential future products, it is helpful not to rely solely on your sales representative. You will need to find a way to talk with the vendor's product development leadership via a customer user group or special working sessions that you ask for.[14]

# Dealing with IT Consultants

Many small- and medium-size organizations have very little if any information technology expertise on staff. When important IT decisions need to be made or when key IT projects arise that need to be executed well, then the use of carefully selected IT consultants could be very helpful and cost-effective.

### Why Use an IT Consultant?

The primary reasons organizations hire IT consultants are:[15]

1. You are making a major software purchase selection and you don't believe you have adequate expertise in that area. For example, you might be purchasing supply chain software for the first time and really don't know the supply chain market place, or what software vendors are good for organizations of your size and business model.

2. Information technology is becoming more important for your organization and you lack IT technical expertise on your staff. For example, you might be a medium to large church and want to put up a new website that serves the needs of your members and people searching for a church.

3. You may have a major IT project arise that you need to implement with excellence and you don't want to hire permanent IT staff for this project. For example, you may be a major health care company with several hospitals, some of which you have recently acquired. And you have chosen to implement a major new hospital information system for all your hospitals and you need to hire IT consultants who can provide the staff to run and manage the projects to implement these systems over the next two years.

### Types of IT Consultants

There are different types of firms that exist in the IT consulting industry.[16]

- Professional services firms that have large professional staffs can do most types of IT work, and are normally fairly expensive. These can be firms such as one of the big accounting firms like Deloitte & Touche or a technical firm such as IBM Global services.
- Staffing firms that primarily provide incremental IT professionals to join your staff temporarily to do very specific projects or tasks.
- Independent consultants of all shapes and sizes that are smaller shops that typically specialize in very specific areas.
- Retired professionals who work through newly developed types of companies (e.g., YourEncore) where technical people make themselves available to do projects in their fields of expertise on a part-time as-needed basis. They come with significant experience and can typically hit the ground running.

And there are hybrid IT consulting firms of all shapes and sizes. Much like choosing a software vendor, be very clear on what you want and how to evaluate and compare alternative consulting firms. Word of mouth referrals and checking references are critical when choosing an IT consulting firm you can trust and work with effectively.

### Fixed versus Variable Priced Consulting Engagements

Most IT consulting firms can do work either at an hourly rate, or for a fixed price for a specific project. There are pros and cons for each type of project. Fixed price contracts have the advantage that you know what you are paying up front, but have the downside of needing to carefully manage the scope of the work being done because any change in the work will require additional costs. Hourly rate types of engagements are good when you don't know the total scope yet and you need the expertise to explore and scope out the work.

# YourEncore Case to Select Critical Packaged Software

As explained earlier in this chapter when we introduced this case, YourEncore is a privately held company with a very innovative business model that has been very successful since their launch in 2003. YourEncore is a company of veteran scientific, engineering, and technical experts that provides clients with solutions based on a lifetime of proven expertise. YourEncore deploys its expertise against capability, capacity, and technical challenges in a confidential environment to help clients develop products essential to healthier, safer, and richer lives.

YourEncore is growing rapidly not only in the United States but across the world. YourEncore has grown from three major clients in 2003 to having over 80 client companies in 2011 and 50 Fortune 1000 clients from primarily the four industry sectors of food, consumer packaged goods, life sciences, and aerospace. YourEncore's existing expert network consists of approximately 6500 veteran professionals, with an average of 25+ years of experience, 67% having advanced degrees, and representing over 1000 companies.

YourEncore needed to replace their existing systems that they use for:

- Project management including time and expense tracking, real-time feedback, and metrics for the over 650 projects done per year for their client companies by experts that YourEncore employs
- Financial functions for the entire firm.

YourEncore's growth in terms of their sales and profits, geographic reach (e.g., 38 states) and worldwide expansion, number of client companies, number of experts in their network, and the types of business alliances they were making, were all factors telling YourEncore top management that their current systems could soon become a barrier to their growth. They wanted to be proactive and move to a single integrated platform where time and expense tracking and their financial systems would be totally integrated together.

YourEncore's existing system for time and expense tracking was a custom built application and their financial system was purchased off

*(Continued)*

the shelf but these two systems were stand-alone and not integrated in any way. Also, because YourEncore has a limited IT professional staff, it was decided that building and supporting their own home-grown integrated set of systems was not a feasible option from a cost and staffing perspective. YourEncore decided to purchase the best integrated time and expense and financial systems they could find in the market.

The first phase of their work to move to a new systems platform was to first analyze their current work processes and simplify them into one common set of core work processes before they automated anything. YourEncore was fortunate to have access to experts from one of their client companies who were Six Sigma experts in analyzing and designing work processes. Their work processes were complex. They focused on the voice of their three types of customers (i.e., internal YE employees, experts/consultants, and client companies). Figure 6.1 shows example work process flows from this work process analysis.

It should be noted that this phase of the project took 18 months to conduct but it was an investment that will pay big dividends, because YourEncore will use systems to leverage and automate new work processes that are built for the future needs of the organization. YourEncore is leveraging better their human capital/headcount by streamlining their work processes and providing improved clarity of job responsibilities. It is not always possible to do this level of work process redesign, but organizations should examine their existing work processes and decide if any significant changes are needed before investing in new information systems to automate these work processes.

The next phase of this project focused on defining the functional requirements that the new software would need to fulfill. Requirements were identified as the project team conducted interviews with the three types of customers mentioned earlier. For example, it was identified that core functionality would include real-time desktop access to data needed to run and manage engagements/projects daily.

Not all requirements are equally important. Critical requirements were identified as those the system must have to be considered. If a system did not perform the critical requirements successfully, it would be eliminated from consideration. Noncritical requirements were also classified as "nice to have" features and would be used to compare alternative software package choices but a system would not

(Continued)

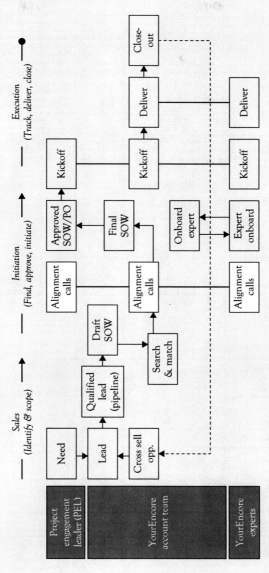

*Figure 6.1. YourEncore work process flows.*

(Continued)

be eliminated if it did not perform these nice to have requirements. Table 6.1 outlines the accounting functional requirements as examples that YourEncore identified.

**Table 6.1. YourEncore Accounting Functional Requirements**

| Use case an interaction between users and system | What primary actions | Who primary users: Expert, hourly OH, sys admin, project admin | Have level must, should, could, would | Deltek response yes no custom |
|---|---|---|---|---|
| Manage clients | | | | |
| Manage data exportation—payroll, electronic billing (EDI) | | | | |
| Manage data importation—payroll, outside transactions, credit card statement download | | | | |
| Manage YourEncore subsidiaries | | | | |
| Manage GL accounts | | | | |
| Manage vendors | | | | |
| Manage payables | | | | |
| Manage credit memos | | | | |
| Process payments | | | | |
| Reconcile account(s) | | | | |
| Lock accounting period(s) | | | | |
| Manage journal voucher(s) | | | | |
| Manage accounts receivable (AR) | | | | |
| Manage payroll | | | | |
| Reimburse expenses | | | | |

(Continued)

*Table 6.1. YourEncore Accounting Functional*
*Requirements—(Continued)*

| | | | | |
|---|---|---|---|---|
| Post time and expenses | | | | |
| Manage profit and loss | | | | |
| Manage balance sheet | | | | |
| Manage cash flow | | | | |
| Manage assets | | | | |
| Manage depreciation | | | | |
| Manage expense categories | | | | |

The next phase of work on this project was to identify potential software vendors and their packages for consideration. The YourEncore team canvassed the vendor market using IT experts, benchmarking with other companies using similar business models, online websites and input from a seasoned IT consultant who had joined the project team and had experience with this type of application software. In total, approximately 15 vendors were looked at.

The project team developed written criteria for the evaluation of the vendor and their software product(s). The core criteria comprised the following:

- Functionality
- Price/costs (included total cost of ownership)
- Implementation risk
- Vendor support
- Feature scalability.

A shortlist of the three top vendors and products was arrived at through detailed evaluation of the 15 potential vendors. Then more rigorous evaluation was used to get down to one vendor. Key pieces of functionality such as level of integration into the financial suite and the functionality of the desktop software eliminated many of the potential vendors. Due diligence of the shortlist of three vendors that got it down to one vendor included financial stability of the vendor's company, customer experiences from references, and the details of provided vendor support for implementation and ongoing

*(Continued)*

maintenance. The final choice made by YourEncore was to select Deltek as the vendor and their Vision package as their new integrated software.

The project team then planned and executed a detailed implementation plan. One of the key implementation decisions YourEncore made was how much historical data from the existing systems to load in the new system. To enable detailed comparisons across time frames, it was decided to load 100% of the financial data for the previous 6.5 years since the company had begun operations.

The implementation project team included most of the project team that had done the work process analysis and selecting the packaged software solution. The team included a project manager (at around 40% full-time equivalent), a full-time IT technical resource, and a business systems manager, as well as a finance resource. The implementation team also included end-users from all levels of users representing the business functions. The implementation of the system took from March to November of 2010. Table 6.2 shows the major milestones for the project plan.

*Table 6.2.* **YourEncore Project Plan**

| Task Name | Start | Finish |
|---|---|---|
| ⊟ **Deltek Vision Implementation** | Tue 12/1/09 | Mon 12/6/10 |
| ⊟ **Phase 1–Project Intiation** | Tue 12/1/09 | Wed 3/31/10 |
| Gather Requirements | Tue 12/1/09 | Thu 12/31/09 |
| Create Project Plan | Thu 3/11/10 | Thu 3/11/10 |
| Consult Deltek for Technical Specs | Mon 12/28/09 | Thu 12/31/09 |
| Create Server Plan | Mon 2/1/10 | Wed 2/10/10 |
| Order Production Servers | Wed 2/10/10 | Wed 3/31/10 |
| Create Cost estimates | Fri 1/1/10 | Tue 1/12/10 |
| Create Scope Of Work with Daasl | Wed 3/10/10 | Mon 3/29/10 |
| ⊟ **Meet with Deltek** | Fri 3/26/10 | Fri 3/26/10 |
| Finalize Sever Configuration and Get Install Guidance | Fri 3/26/10 | Fri 3/26/10 |
| ⊞ **Phase 2–Solution Design** | Wed 3/10/10 | Mon 7/5/10 |
| ⊞ **Phase 3–Configuration & Construction** | Wed 3/10/10 | Thu 9/23/10 |
| ⊞ **Phase 4–Deployment Readiness** | Wed 6/9/10 | Thu 11/25/10 |
| ⊞ **Phase 5–Go Live and Stabilization** | Fri 11/26/10 | Mon 12/6/10 |

## Lessons Learned

The major lessons learned that this case illustrates are:

1. Be proactive if you can, change before you have to or are forced.
2. Examine your work processes first before you select and implement your software.

*(Continued)*

3. Be realistic about the time (both elapsed time and effort) this effort will take.

4. Consider the medium- to long-term aspects of your software selection. Consider the total cost of ownership and how to leverage your new system capabilities.

5. Formally identify and document your system requirements by asking your customers what they need—"the voice of the customer."

6. Build a good project team with the right technical expertise and experience as well as an excellent project manager who has experience with IT projects. If you don't have these people on your staff, consider hiring consultants who do have these skills.

7. Document the criteria you will use to evaluate your potential vendors.

8. Conduct thorough due diligence of your shortlist of potential vendors.

9. Employ proven IT project management best practices.

10. Consider the burden and costs on your existing internal resources to execute this type of project because this project will require additional work and it could be a distraction from the day-to-day operations. There is no "good time" for this type of major implementation project so find ways to keep your daily work moving, including selective use of temporary help.

Tim Tichenor, Chief Financial Officer

Shannon Johnson, Manager Business Processes

YourEncore, Inc.

# How Information Technology Can Help Achieve Competing Objectives

## *Executives Setting Strategy and Managers Implementing It*

Enterprise architecture is itself a strategic planning exercise. This exercise considers your business objectives and lays out a practical transition plan from your current situation to the defined future state of how IT is deployed and used. This future state of IT enables you to implement your future business strategy and achieve your business goals. Implementing the transition plan is the key action to achieving the benefits you have predicted. The transition plan is a series of projects to be implemented with excellence.

When IT provides new capabilities or functionality, this often enables business transformation to take place. How work gets done in the future work processes given these new capabilities can be designed in radically new ways. This provides both new ways of doing work as well as better ways of doing the things you already do in less time, with fewer people, and with better results.

IT is pervasive—it is everywhere helping people carry out tasks. As you make changes to your operation(s), you must make tactical changes to your IT applications to effect the changes you are making.

Therefore, enterprise architecture does enable strategy to be both better formulated and implemented.

### Sustainable Organizational Capability and Achieving Current Business Results

IT is all about building capability. Investing in new and upgraded information systems is primarily building new capability for your organization. IT provides opportunities to do work in the future in dramatically different ways that deliver tangible business benefits.

Using IT is typically enabling organizations to leverage their scale and improve the productivity of their people to achieve current business results in more effective ways.

Therefore the careful use of information technology can build organizational capability as well as delivering current business results.

### Project Goals and Operational Goals

First, let us explain the difference. Project goals are measurable milestones achieved in the project schedule, while operational goals are achieving levels of performance in executing your current day-to-day operations, such as production volume or finished product quality targets.

It is clear that operational goals are most often achieved with the help of automation through information systems. Project goals are typically time and cost measures of how well a project is executed. Project management software tools are frequently very helpful in reaching these measures. However, project goals could be new operational goal levels achieved only through the new IT capabilities being implemented in the project.

In this case, IT systems would often be part of what the project is implementing that would enable these new levels of performance.

### One Function's Goals and Another Function's Goals

Organizations, by their very nature, are multifunctional, where functions are defined as disciplines such as sales, manufacturing, research and development, etc. Information systems, especially enterprise-wide systems like CRM and enterprise resource planning (ERP), impact work processes that cross many functions. As these enterprise-wide systems enable new business benefits, they help functions achieve their goals, typically improved operational performance levels. Therefore these types of systems allow an organization to achieve goals from many functions at the same time.

## Top 10 Information Technology Assessment Questions

1. How critical is your IT (information technology) function to the success of your organization? How do you know?
2. How strategic is IT in your industry and/or with your prime competitors? How do you know?
3. Where is your organization on the IT adoption model? That is, are you a leader? Are you a fast follower? Or are you a laggard?
4. How do you stay up to date on new advances in IT that may be relevant to your organization or industry?
5. Do you buy versus build your software solutions/applications? Why?
6. What is your next strategic IT application project in the next year?
7. Have you evaluated the potential impact of social media applications on the Web on your organization? If not, why not?
8. What categories of data/information are most important for your organization?
9. What is your IT master plan for the next 1–3 years? If you don't have one, how would you develop one?
10. How do you proactively develop and maintain important relationships with your key IT vendors? If you don't, what should you begin doing with which vendor(s) to get started?

# APPENDIX B

# Technology Basics

## Software

The two major types of software are application software and systems software. An application (often called an "App" in the current Apple iPad jargon) is a computer program designed to do a specific set of tasks (e.g., process payroll checks, find a restaurant, pay an invoice, etc.) or support a set of business processes such as providing resumes and job postings for the recruiting processes in the human resources function of a company.

Applications can range from a very specific program for your Blackberry, iPad, or personal computer to do very specific things (e.g., track stock prices) to global enterprise-wide sets of applications that automate hundreds of cross-company work processes like your supply chain termed enterprise resource planning (ERP) or software for your entire sales function, often called customer relationship management systems (CRM). Application software is the area of IT that people care the most about because they are the programs that do something!

Systems software is the class of computer programs that sit on top and work with the computer hardware to run or execute your application programs. These consist of programs called operating systems that control the hardware components of your computer (processor, main memory, disk storage, etc.) and have names like Vista or XP for your IBM Windows personal computer or Mac OS X (stands for the Macintosh operating system version 10) for the Apple Mac computers. Systems software also includes language compilers that enable application programs written in different computer languages (e.g., C, Perl, JAVA, or Python) to execute or run on various types of computer hardware.[17] There are also software programs that provide basic tools that enable the user to do meaningful work that can be tailored to do exactly what they need. Examples are word processors and spreadsheet programs.

The last basic concepts on software that we need to cover are software versions and software upgrades. Software programs, both applications and systems software, over time, have new versions designed, written, and released commercially. Typically, a new version of a software application (or an operating system for that matter) is produced with new and additional features in mind (computer folks also call this additional "functionality") as well as fixing known problems (or "bugs") with the existing software version. These new versions are therefore often called "upgrades." The naming conventions for versions can be rather cryptic at times. A major version or software release will often be a whole number such as version 5.0 (read 5 point oh). While a minor upgrade will often just advance a tenth, that is, to go from version 5.0 to version 5.1 would indicate a minor version upgrade. Major and minor upgrades indicate how much new capability has been added to the software—a lot or a little. Upgrades can be free or be priced separately or be included in your annual software maintenance contract. In some instances, it may be smart to **skip** a version upgrade if the cost is significant and the capability being added is of little or no interest.

## Hardware

It does help to "demystify" what computers do and how they are built. Computers (of any size) have the following generic components:[18]

- The central processing unit (CPU) is the "brains" of the computer. The CPU directs and controls the tasks done by the other components and moves and manages the data needed to perform the tasks being done.
- Input devices allow data and programs to be input into the computer and converted to a form that the computer can understand.
- Output devices take data and information and present it to people in forms that they can understand.
- Primary storage is an area that allows the computer to temporarily store data and programs while it is being worked on. It is like intermediate storage for "work in progress."

- Secondary storage is the ability of the computer to store large volumes of data over long periods of time for future use and access.
- Communication devices enable data and programs to flow across computer networks that link computers together either physically or virtually.

## Telecommunications

The diagram below illustrates the concept of connectivity by showing devices (computers, PDAs, fax, phone, etc.) that communicate over different types of media (Wi-Fi, cable, satellite, microwave, etc.) via purchased services from telecommunications companies such as AT&T, or Verizon.[19]

Detailed pros and cons for each media based on costs and capabilities are beyond the scope of this book. However, it is important to note that data transmission over a coaxial cable that is digital is called broadband. It can carry multiple signals simultaneously and is fast for high-volume use and is therefore the most popular Internet access method. Bandwidth is the common measure for network capacity that tells you how much data per second can be transmitted over a given size of network. To use a plumbing analogy, how large a pipe is, is the capacity of how much water you can pump, how fast through a pipe.

Mobile devices have exploded in their use across the world and one of the compelling reasons is their ability to easily communicate across both wireless and physical networks.

The technologies of telecommunications and networking depend on the use of communication standards and common network protocols. To connect millions of devices together, everyone needs to use the same standards that allow you to communicate with one another.

A common standard you may hear referenced when talking about communicating over the Internet (we will explain the Internet in more depth in a coming section) is called Transmission Control Protocol/Internet Protocol (TCP/IP). It enables error free transmission between various systems over computer networks and is the standard transmission method used on the Internet.

There also exist private networks that organizations may find cost-effective to install and maintain. They are local area networks (LAN) and wide area networks (WAN). A local area network enables two or more devices to communicate with one another over a relatively short distance (e.g., a few thousand feet). Every user device on the LAN has the ability to communicate with every other device. LANs are normally used to connect devices within an organization. LANs can be physically connected together. A LAN allows a large number of users to share common resources like printers, storage, and common programs.

Wide area networks on the other hand are broadband technology often covering long distances. They typically cross rights-of-way where communication media are provided by common carriers commercially. WANs can be privately owned or commercially provided networks that are regulated. WANs are both regional and international in potential scope. Companies that have locations in many countries will certainly have either private or purchased WAN capability. Figure 6B.1 is an illustration of networks.

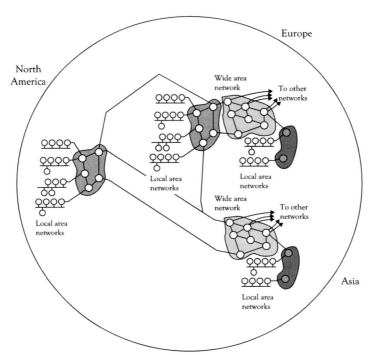

*Figure 6B.1. Global connectivity (LANs and WANs).*

There are many measures related to computer networks but the most useful measure is bandwidth or capacity—in other words how many characters per second capacity does this network provide. You may remember in the early days of personal computers logging on to a network with 300 KB (kilobit) per second speed (or 300,000 characters per second). Today fiber optic networks operate at far higher speeds, in the 8-Gbit per second range (or 8 billion characters per second).

## Internet 1.0 and 2.0

It is useful to think of the two generations that the Internet has gone through in the past 10 years. The first generation, sometimes called Internet 1.0, was primarily a static compilation of information—like an online library of information. This was a huge breakthrough and allowed information to be shared with billions of people around the world.[20]

As people have used and leveraged the Internet, a new generation of usage of the Internet has emerged, called Internet 2.0. While Internet 1.0 was an online library of information, Internet 2.0 is like having a shared canvas where people from around the world can participate in mass collaboration to create a beautiful picture together. This now enables a dramatically different type of use of the Internet. This is the era we are now experiencing as we see thousands of apps being made available over mobile and tablet devices.

## Databases

Enterprise software that manages the creation, use, and ongoing maintenance of databases is called database management systems (DBMS). Oracle and IBM are two of the major DBMS vendors. Microsoft Access is a DBMS but on a much smaller scale for smaller organizations.

These databases stored in a DBMS are typically centralized and accessed by applications that need access to this data and/or produce data to be stored in these databases.

DBMS allows people to define, and populate databases, and then to analyze, and report on data/information contained in these databases. (See chapter 5 for data-based decision making—databases are where the data come from to make these types of decisions.)

Examples of databases often defined and used in industry are customer databases where information about your customers is stored, product databases where detailed information about your products is stored, and transactional information such as a shipment database that keeps track of all the shipments made during a given time period, including what products were shipped, to what customer, at what price.

Databases can contain many different types of data. Quantitative information and textual descriptions are quite common. But one can also store diagrams, pictures, images, even audio recordings and video clips. Storing many different types of information is becoming common.

One aspect of defining a database is defining the logical model or how you want the data to be organized. These are called logical models because they embody the basic logic used to organize the data in the database. There is a corresponding physical model in designing a database but it has more to do with how to optimize the actual performance of the database management software that stores and retrieves the data.

A key concept that you need to understand in defining a logical database is the concept of a key data element. A key is a data element that once you know its value (e.g., student number) you can determine unique values for other nonkey data. In this example below,[21] once you know the student number for a person, you can then relate this student number to unique and distinct value for nonkey data elements such as student name, student address, year in school, etc.

As you can see from this simple example, key data elements are powerful and are very important in defining what data you want stored and how that data is logically organized. The collection of all of your key data elements is called master data. Master data is an important set of data to

Table 6B.1. Student Data Table

| Student # (Key) | Student name | Student street address | Student city | Student state | Student zip code | Student year in school |
|---|---|---|---|---|---|---|
|  |  |  |  |  |  |  |
|  |  |  |  |  |  |  |
|  |  |  |  |  |  |  |

define for an organization because it determines so much other data that is important to the organization. Master data is also the way multiple types of data get linked together and integrated together, which is very important in looking at and analyzing collections of data.

In the logical database world, vendors or consultants may use the following terms when talking about databases. There are three basic logical model types that people consider:

1. Hierarchical model
2. Network model
3. Relational model.

We will **not** go into greater detail on these three types of data models because that could get very complex and is not required for most business leaders. What you do need to understand is that the relational model is basically a set of 2-dimensional tables and is often the type of data model vendors will use to talk with you about their products. These tables are easy for people to understand and visualize their data. Having this understanding enables users to write queries for the data to be extracted as well as defining useful reports for use in the organization.

## Level of Detail and Data Volumes

One decision that you will need to make is at what level of detail and how much history will you keep and store your transactional data. For example, in storing shipment transaction data, you could choose to store each shipment by date and for each stock keeping unit (SKU) by customer. Or, you could summarize the shipment data by customer by summarizing all the shipment volume for each day, or you could summarize the data by customer by week or by month. Once you make the level of detail determination, you will then need to decide whether you will keep 2 years of history, 4 years of history, or the exact period of time you need historical/past data for.

The implications of these decisions need to be understood. I normally recommend you store transaction data at the lowest level of detail that it naturally occurs. Once you summarize data, you lose forever the lower level detail that you have summarized. The other implication is how much data in terms of volume (gigabytes) you will be storing. This is simple mathematics for how many characters will be stored once you know how many transactions and for how many years you will be storing your data.

# APPENDIX C

# Architecture Global Standard

## A Global Standard—TOGAF (The Open Group Architecture Framework)

Having a defined and widely adopted standard methodology for doing enterprise IT architecture is an important breakthrough in this area. It means that there is an agreed upon method for developing an enterprise IT architecture and that learnings can be shared using a common set of terminology and frameworks. The Open Group has developed and published a global standard architecture methodology called TOGAF, which stands for The Open Group Architecture Framework.[22] TOGAF is defined in their terms as follows.

"The Open Group is a vendor-neutral and technology-neutral consortium, whose vision of Boundaryless Information Flow™ will enable access to integrated information, within and among enterprises, based on open standards and global interoperability."

"TOGAF is a comprehensive framework and methodology which enables the design, evaluation and implementation of the right architecture for an enterprise."

TOGAF is illustrated in Figure 6C.1.[23] For more information, please visit www.opengroup.org.

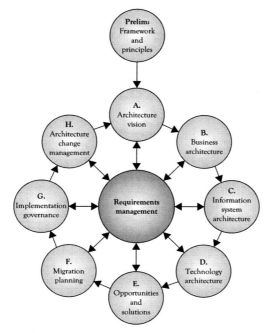

*Figure 6C.1. The open group architecture framework.*

## The Role of Standards

In the computer and information technology area there are literally hundreds of standards. Standards exist in hardware, software, telecommunications, database management, and throughout the use of computers including methodologies to support them and fix problems (e.g., ITIL—information technology infrastructure library used for IT service management). The concept of a standard is simple, to identify a specific design, way of doing something, protocol, format, etc. and label that as a specific standard so that when they see that standard name, people know exactly what it means by knowing the definition of that standard. The purpose of standards is to enable things to be built in such a way that they interoperate or work together with few or no issues.[24]

The acronym soup that you can create by listing software standards for example can cause great confusion for business leaders who are not deep into computer technology (e.g., HTML, TCP/IP, SMTP, POP, and FTP).

The real question we need to answer is "What do I need to know as a business professional about computer standards?" First, you need to know that they exist and that in most cases, standards are good because they make things work well together now and in the future. Second, when you are buying or leasing computer hardware or software, you need to ask, what are the important and strategic standards that exist in this area? And does this product or service comply with these standards?

Standards are typically set by independent (of vendors) organizations who maintain and publish these standards. Standards do change and evolve over time so you will need to know exactly which version of the standards you are talking about.

The other use of standards is that many organizations make strategic selections from across the wide variety of IT products and then communicate and publish that these are the organization's standards and will be used unless an exception is granted. For example standardizing on an electronic mail package, word processor, and spreadsheet software, are common to allow everyone in an organization to communicate with one another and share common documents and spreadsheets in formats that everyone can read.

Standards allow organizations to leverage their scale and control their costs by having as few options as they can to get their work done. This reduced complexity is very helpful in enabling change in the future when capability is added, since you will only have to change the few standard choices you have made.[25]

## Open versus Closed Standards

As if the IT world isn't complex enough, there are differences between open and closed standards. An open standard, as the name implies, is documented and available to the public and anyone. Then anyone can create a product or service that adheres to this published open standard. LINUX is an open standard operating system that any vendor can develop and can introduce a computer that uses it.

On the other hand, a closed standard is owned and developed usually by a specific vendor. That vendor often controls who can produce products that adhere to that standard and may even charge people to use the standard. Usually products built on a closed standard have dominant market share and that is what motivates vendors to want to develop products that follow these closed standards. A prime example of widely used closed standards is the Microsoft Office file format standards of .doc for documents and .xls for spreadsheets.

# APPENDIX D

# Commercial Software Basics

## Customer User Groups

Application software vendors most often have a customer user group organization that is established by the software vendor to provide a way for current customers to network with one another and learn from each other's experiences. To be clear, it is a marketing oriented activity as well as a way for customers to input their future needs to the vendor for consideration in being addressed in a future release of the software.

I strongly encourage organizations that have made a commitment to an application software vendor to become active in that vendor's customer user group! In fact, I would also encourage prospective customers to attend a customer user group meeting **before** they make a purchase commitment so they can get input from current customers and see how the vendor operates and what their impression is of how this vendor works with their customers. This will be very useful information to consider when evaluating possible vendor choices.

## Contracts

It is beyond the scope of this book to go into great detail how to negotiate and establish contractual relationships with application software vendors. But from years of experience when dealing with application software vendors, there are a few basic points that will prove to be very helpful to understand.

1. Software companies have high margins and their marketing people are normally very aggressive and willing to deal, especially near the end of their (the vendor's) fiscal year! Do not be bashful in asking for special accommodations.

2. It is imperative you get your strategic purchasing manager (if you have one) involved in contract discussions as early as possible. They are professionals in this area and can save you much money and time. **If** you do not have such a resource on your staff, this is an area where a consultant specializing in software selection and contracts could be a very wise choice.

3. A common practice in the software industry is to have your annual maintenance fee be a fixed percentage (e.g., 10%) of the purchase cost. So, if the software cost you $50,000, the annual maintenance fee could be $5000 per year. Make sure you understand these clauses. Annual maintenance for software normally includes new software releases, providing support for the product, and reporting and fixing problems. Some training may also be included.

# CHAPTER 7

# Making Sensible Decisions Using Data: A Responsibility of All Executives

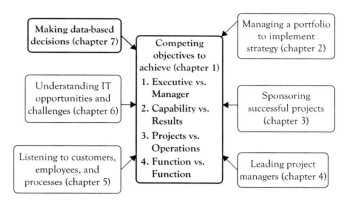

This chapter focuses on one of the key quality management principles discussed in chapter 5, data-based decision making. This chapter deals with the analyses of both quantitative and qualitative data and its synthesis with human judgment to make good decisions. We believe helping people make data-based decisions will positively impact each executive role we listed in chapter 1. The purpose of this chapter is to:

- Understand why making decisions based on data is so key to an organization.
- Learn how to define and collect high quality data.

- Learn basic and moderately complex quantitative data analysis techniques and how to gain insight from their use.
- Learn why qualitative data is important as well for making decisions.
- Learn basic and moderately complex qualitative data analysis techniques and how to gain insight from their use.
- Learn how and when to integrate both quantitative and qualitative data to make decisions.
- Understand what standards exist globally for data analysis techniques and tools.

Organizations make hundreds of decisions every day. What is the big deal about decisions being based on data? The opposite of making decisions based on data is making decisions based on what you think is true, or what you think is the current situation, or just simply what the decision-maker wants to do. This can lead to very poor outcomes. Data-based decisions mean that you define and collect objective, accurate, and current data (both quantitative and qualitative) that describes what the current situation **actually** is. You allow the data to speak and give you insights as you analyze the data using valid and proven analysis techniques.

An organization that follows data-based decision making actually empowers its people to make significant contributions. This is done because people at all levels and seniority in the organization know that if they can collect and analyze the data surrounding an issue or a problem, the conclusions they draw and the recommendations they make will be listened to and acted upon. This is a tremendous asset for an organization.

It must be noted that following this principle does not mean that intangible or political factors cannot be considered in making complex decisions. It just means that you need to include objective analysis of the data relevant for a decision and factor this insight into the decision being made.

# Givaudan Case—Making Research Portfolio Decisions

Givaudan is a global leader in the fragrance and flavor industry, offering its products to global, regional and local food, beverage, consumer goods, and fragrance companies. Their Flavour Division has four business units: Beverages, Dairy, Savoury, and Sweet Goods. The Fragrance Division has three business units: Fine Fragrances, Consumer Products, and Fragrance Ingredients.

Headquartered in Vernier, Switzerland, Givaudan holds a 25% market share in an industry that is valued overall at around CHF 17 billion. They have been listed on the SIX Swiss Exchange since June 2000 and are one of the country's 30 largest companies in terms of market capitalization. In 2010, Givaudan achieved sales of CHF 4.2 billion, with a workforce of over 8600 employees and subsidiaries in 45 countries. It has a presence in all major markets and a network of 82 sites in mature and developing regions.

They invest more in research and development than any other company in the industry and have the heritage, scale, and the supply chain to serve worldwide customers seamlessly with innovative products and concepts. The problem they have, like many successful corporations, is they have more good ideas for new products than they have money and people to work on them. This case illustrates how Givaudan uses both quantitative and qualitative factors to make tough R&D portfolio decisions.

**The key question facing Givaudan leaders** "Does the culture of your organization support the widespread use of data-based decision making?"

# Defining and Collecting High Quality Data

The logical question when posed with an important decision to make is, what data do I need or can I get to help us make this decision? It is helpful to distinguish what are called **in-process measures** from **outcome**

**measures**. These two types of measures are best understood in the context of work processes. If you consider the YourEncore case study from chapter 6 on information technology, we can look at the work processes used to manage an expert engagement. Let's simplify the process to the following steps:

1. A client approaches YourEncore account manager with a request for a project.
2. YourEncore works with the client to draft a statement of work (SOW).
3. Based on the SOW, a set of expert skills and experience is identified.
4. YourEncore searches its expert database to identify expert candidates. It then presents the top three to five expert candidates to the client for their selection and schedules an alignment call with a candidate expert.
5. Once a match is made where the expert is available and has the right skills and the client wants them to do the work, a formal project engagement is formed.

For this process, some example in-process measures are:

- Number of candidate experts identified with the requested skills.
- Elapsed time in days it takes from the date of initial request until the project is staffed and begun.
- Number of client leads where a request is made.
- What percentage of client leads end up in actual contracted projects.

For this same process, some example outcome measures are:

- Financial measures for completed projects such as
  - Total dollars billed
  - Profit booked

- Customer satisfaction (subjective measure from 1 to 7)
- Quantitative benefits achieved by the project such as rate of return or net present value.

### Collecting High Quality Data

It is preferred if you can collect data from your information systems if the data you want are actually being stored in the computer applications used to run your business. However, sometimes the data you need for a study will require at least some of the data to be collected manually or with special computer programs to collect data that are not normally collected in your systems.

If you are collecting data manually, you will need to define a form or what is sometimes called a check sheet to collect the data you want.[1] Figure 7.1 below shows a simple check sheet used to collect consumer comments that are received at a call center for a bank. Call centers often use automated systems to track their performance, so it would be likely that consumer comments are already tracked by the call center in their problem tracking system. However, if comments are not tracked, Figure 7.1 lays out a simple form used to collect this data. Note that there is one sheet for each consumer comment. Therefore, there is a need to summarize this raw data by shift, by date, by type of comment, etc.

Issues that need to be considered are what event/transaction are you collecting and how much data, and exactly what data will be collected? For example, do you want to know the exact time of day when each comment was tracked, or is having consumer comments grouped by 8-hour shifts sufficient level of detail? For the type of comment, do you have

| Type of comment: (Circle one or fillout other) | Date _____ Shift _____ |
|---|---|
| CH—Complaint re: Checking account SV—Complaint re: Saving account LN—Complaint re: Loan CO—Complaint for good service Other (explain) _____ | Verbatim comments: |

*Figure 7.1. Check sheet for consumer comments.*

a finite list of choices and one "Other" category? Or do you allow people to write in freeform text to explain those comments that do not match one of the choices provided? The form has to be as clear as possible so it can be consistently used.[2]

A useful concept is to define in writing exactly what you mean by each data element that you are collecting. This written definition is called the **operational definition**. For example, the operational definition of a consumer comment could be: "When a consumer of our products calls our 800 numbers, we will categorize the nature of why they are calling based on the developed standard list of types of consumer comments we typically receive. If a consumer calls with a comment that does not match a predefined type, we record the comment as other and then record the actual words or verbatim of that comment." Now this is not a perfect definition but does reflect the level of precision needed when writing a good operational definition.

It is helpful to consider the types of quality attributes you should strive to achieve as you collect data, either via information systems or manually collected. Common attributes that are helpful are timely, accurate, clear, consistent, and relevant.

## Analyzing Quantitative Data

In today's world, most quantitative analytical techniques are automated and provide fast and accurate capabilities. However, it is important often to understand the basic intent or approach for an analytical technique that is embedded in the software. In this book, the underlying logic and mechanics for relevant quantitative methods are included in Appendix E.

The techniques included in Appendix E are:

- Simple graphs and measures
- Simple statistics, probability, and uncertainty measures (includes confidence intervals)
- Trends and patterns (histograms, Pareto charts)
- Time series forecasting (moving averages, exponential smoothing).

## Decision Analysis

Decision analysis techniques represent ways to make decisions when a decision-maker is faced with several alternatives and the future events have uncertainty or risk associated with them. Part of the beauty of decision analysis approaches is how decisions are structured.[3]

When formulating a problem, you need to identify the "decision alternatives," as well as what are called "states of nature" that describe the uncertain future. Let's take an example of building apartments in the new Banks project in downtown Cincinnati. Table 7.1 is a payoff table that shows the expected payoff or net profit for each combination of a decision alternative and a state of nature. In this case, the decision alternatives are to build a **small** development of **50 units** ($d_1$), a **medium** development of **100 units** ($d_2$), or a **large** development with **150 units** ($d_3$). Two states of nature are identified. They are strong demand for condominiums (s1) or having weak demand for condominiums (s2). Table 7.1 shows the expected payoffs/net profits for those six combinations.

It is often helpful to visually depict this decision situation using what is called a decision tree, as seen in Figure 7.2. Decision trees enable people to decompose problems into sequential steps. Large complex decisions can be formulated by being decomposed into a series of smaller sub-problems.

The only thing missing now is getting information on how likely is each state of nature. In other words, what is the probability that there will be strong demand for condominiums in this area? Once we estimate these state of nature probabilities, we can calculate what is called the **expected value for each decision alternative**.

You can calculate the expected value using the data in the payoff table in Table 7.1, and the newly estimated probabilities (0.80 for strong demand and therefore 0.20 for weak demand). Therefore, the expected values are calculated as:

$$Ev(d_1) = 0.8(11) + 0.2(10) = 10.8$$
$$Ev(d_2) = 0.8(17) + 0.2(8) = 15.2$$
$$Ev(d_3) = 0.8(23) + 0.2(-6) = 17.2$$

*Table 7.1. Payoff Table for Apartments at the Banks Project in Cincinnati (Payoffs in $ Million)*

| State of Nature | | |
|---|---|---|
| **Decision atternative** | **Strong demand ($S_1$)** | **Weak demand ($S_2$)** |
| Small Complex ($d_1$) | 11 | 10 |
| Medium Complex ($d_2$) | 17 | 8 |
| Large Complex ($d_3$) | 23 | –6 |

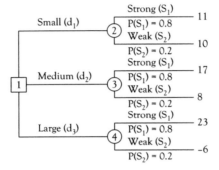

*Figure 7.2. Decision tree for apartments at the BANKS project in Cincinnati (Payoffs in $ Million).*

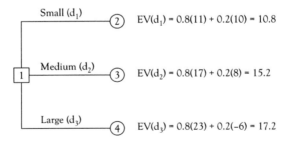

*Figure 7.3. Cincinnati apartments project expected values.*

Looking at these expected values, we choose the decision alternative that gives us the largest expected value, which is d3 or building a large complex of 150 units. We can add this expected value to the decision tree as seen in Figure 7.3. This is a compact graphical way to depict all the necessary data involved in calculating the expected value approach for decision analysis.

## Qualitative Data Analyses

We use the term qualitative data to distinguish it from quantitative data where the variable takes on a numeric value. Qualitative data can come in many flavors including **categorical data**, textual responses to questions, as well as ideas and other meaningful observations where their value is not a number that has a physical meaning.

See Appendix E for use of simple bar charts and pie charts as a way to graph your data to visualize what is going on.

### Surveys

Survey design is a large and detailed subject. We will cover the very basics in this section so you are able to consider collecting and using this type of qualitative information. Surveys are useful ways to collect information such as ideas, opinions, levels of satisfaction, and feelings.[4] Surveys can collect information from a wide cross-section of people at a relatively low cost. Especially now with web-based tools to construct and widely distribute surveys online, surveys can be used effectively.

Surveys are often used to create useful sample information to make conclusions about the larger population being observed. Classic surveys are Gallup polls or TV watching surveys to create insight on overall behavior of the population as a whole. Therefore, surveys need to be representative and have a large enough sample size to be worthwhile.

A useful example would be if you inherited a successful radio station: you may want to survey your listeners to see why they listen, what they like about your station, and what they think you could improve.

Some basic tips on useful survey design are:

- Define the objective of the survey and identify what information you plan to collect to achieve this objective

- Do not use biased wording that can skew your responses
- Recognize that a low % return could be a problem. Less than 25% returned could be biased negatively.
- For a survey, consistently use the same 3- or 5- or 7-point scale for responses.
- You can use multiple-choice questions
- You can use yes/no and explain questions
- You can use open-ended questions to explore areas not well understood.

## Interviews

Interviews are more intensive, normally done face-to-face, and can collect more in-depth information.

Interviews are often only as good as the person conducting the interviews. Interviews can be a useful step in talking with key decision-makers to understand what key issues they believe need to be looked at when examining a business situation. Structured interviews with key people can collect key information and identify key themes and trends.[5] Detailed design and validation of interviews and how to conduct effective interviews are beyond the scope of this text.

## Affinity Diagrams

The affinity diagram is a very powerful technique for grouping large numbers of complex ideas, opinions, and issues that may at first appear unrelated into meaningful groupings that are displayed visually.[6,7] This analysis technique is very useful with groups of people, getting their input and collective knowledge to understand the nature of a problem and to identify key ideas and action items. This technique requires both logical and creative forms of thinking. It depends on effective teamwork that values different perspectives. (This is also known as the KJ Method developed in the 1960s in Japan). The detailed steps to construct an affinity diagram are included in Appendix F (Figure 7.4).

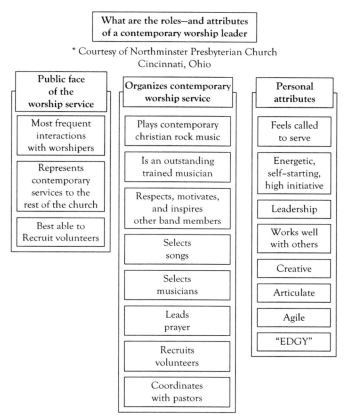

*Figure 7.4. Affinity diagram.*

## Interrelationship Diagraphs

This is a graphical technique that analyzes the cause and effect relationships between a problem or issue and the factors that may be causing it. The interrelationship diagraph is often used with an affinity diagram as a first step to identify the key factors relating to an issue or problem. However, this technique requires a smaller team of people, ideally four to six people maximum, and an in-depth knowledge of the subject matter to assess potential cause and effect relationships.

The power of this technique is that, if applied thoughtfully, it will identify root causes/key drivers for a problem or issue. It will also identify

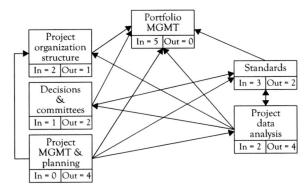

*Figure 7.5. Inter-relationship diagraph—areas of opportunities.*

both primary and secondary causes of a given effect, and determine in what order issues need to be addressed to remedy the problem or issue. This technique dissects the complexity of an issue and shows that there may be, in fact, a number of factors at play that have a nonlinear relationship to each other.[8,9] Details on the steps to construct an interrelationship diagraph are included in Appendix F.

Figure 7.5 illustrates a typical interrelationship diagram format for opportunities for an organization to do better project management. Both Project Data Analysis and Project Management & Planning have the most number of out arrows and this identifies these as the key drivers. Portfolio management is the effect.

### Delphi Technique

The Delphi technique is a structured and interactive communication process with a panel of experts typically used for forecasting and policy development. It was developed in the 1950s by the Rand Corporation and is based on the assumption that the collective judgment of a group of experts is more accurate than individual judgments. It continues to be used today for forecasting uncertain futures with selected experts. It is a useful technique for qualitative data and expert opinion and that is why it is included in this chapter.

A key aspect of the Delphi technique is that all the responses remain anonymous throughout the process and after the process is completed. This enables each person's opinion to have equal weight.[10]

The standard version of the Delphi technique works as follows:

1. Choose your panel of experts. These people should have relevant deep expertise in areas related to what you are trying to forecast or develop. Having a cross-section of people from areas of relevant expertise is preferred.
2. Using a questionnaire or other structured instrument, obtain forecasts from all panel members. Their responses need to include their rationale on key assumptions and issues related to their forecasts.
3. Summarize the responses/forecasts and redistribute them to all panel members with the rationales. You also ask the next set of questions.
4. Usually three rounds are sufficient to get convergence to a collective forecast.
5. Repeat iterations past three rounds if needed to gain reasonable consensus.

The person organizing and conducting the Delphi technique is called the facilitator. This person selects the experts, develops the questionnaires, sends and receives the panelist's forecasts and rationale, and summarizes the responses and sends them to the panel for the next round.

The Delphi Technique can incorporate multiple criteria used by the experts to select among choices to reach a consensus in a complex area.[11]

## Multivoting

Multivoting is a very common technique used in many total quality and group methods. There are several variations to how multivoting is conducted. It is basically asking a group of people to vote on what they think are the most important items based on some criteria that the group understands.

For example, a project team lists 10 major potential risks for their project. The team is then asked to vote on these 10 items based on which risks they believe are the most important to have mitigation plans for. A standard round of multivoting would look like this:

1. Divide the number of total items in half and that becomes the number of votes each person gets. In this case, each person gets 5 votes.
2. Then you specify the voting rules. One option is to allow people to spend all their votes on one item if they feel that strongly about it. Another option is to restrict voting by stating that you cannot place more than one vote on any item.
3. People would then cast their votes based on the declared voting rules and the votes would be counted and the top item(s) identified.
4. Multiple rounds of voting can be used if you have a large number of items to be voted on. In each round, you start with step 1 above.

## Global Standards

Unlike the areas of project management and total quality, there are no well-accepted global standards for quantitative and qualitative data analysis methods. The closest this area comes to standards are using standard software packages to run common statistical calculations, for example. Packages like SAS and SPSS can be adopted as standard tools to make sure that when a standard deviation is calculated, it is done the same way throughout the world.

## Making Good Decisions

Making good decisions consists of using all the data you have at your disposal, applying selected quantitative and qualitative analysis techniques, and synthesizing those results with the political reality of the situation to make the best call you can. You will see this at work in the Givaudan case.

## Givaudan Case—Portfolio Decisions

As introduced earlier in this chapter, this case illustrates how Givaudan uses both quantitative and qualitative factors to make tough R&D portfolio decisions. Because of the confidentiality of Givaudan's R&D portfolio, the case presents hypothetical product examples but does

*(Continued)*

illustrate the type of process that is used to make these types of R&D portfolio decisions.

## Overview of the Process

Two independent research portfolios are established and managed: one research portfolio for the Flavors Division and another research portfolio for the Fragrances division. To limit the scope of the case, we are focusing only on the Flavors research portfolio. Projects in this Flavors research portfolio span business units (i.e., beverages, dairy, savory, and sweet goods). Reapplying insights across business units is a primary reason that each business unit does not have its own research portfolio.

The process to select and execute a set of research projects to fund and execute is actually fairly simple.

A full set of potential research projects are identified and written down by research management. A set of weighted criteria are established that will be used to evaluate each research project. In this example, five research criteria are used. The weight or how relatively important this criteria is has been determined by research management.

## Establishing the Criteria

A key observation was that given interest rates are so low for a business where the margins are higher than the cost of borrowing, having criteria beyond financial criteria is very important to decide between projects.

Since some criteria are financial and some criteria are technical in nature; not all people vote on all criteria. Financial people vote on the financial criteria because they are very knowledgeable in this area and can give very valid assessments. Similarly, research scientists vote on technical criteria of which they are very knowledgeable.

Considerations for possible criteria include:

- Devise a series of questions designed to get each participant to differentiate projects based on their knowledge base.
- It is worth spending time with the project reviewers to make sure all people understand the criteria in the same way and these criteria are important decision criteria.

(Continued)

- Use values of 0, 1, 3, and 9 and explain what each score means for that criterion. Make sure 9 is the most preferred value for each criterion.

Five example criteria which might be used to make project decisions are shown in the following table.

| Guiding principle | Functionality | How to fill out | Weight |
|---|---|---|---|
| Achieves | Solves a known problem and/or contributes to our core competencies that are strategic to the future Success of the company (foundational). | 9 = Completely 3 = In Part 1= Unlikely 0 = Not at all | 5 |
| Feasibility | Probability of Technical Success—take into account regulatory/safety feasibility risk. If we have mature knowledge in house already or available through a consultant and operational feasibility. | Chances of success are: 9 = High 3 = Medium 1 = Low 0 = Nonexistant | 3 |
| Feasibility | Project Cost of Resources vs. Forecast Sales Ratio | 9 = >1:10 5 = 1:5 3 = 1:1 1 = up to 2:1 0 = >2:1 | 7 |
| Value | Fits Givaudan Strategic Plan and increases Market Attractiveness/Retention—the product is differentiating in uniqueness, cost or quality. | This project involves products or processes which fits the strategic plan and will grow current business, enable entry into new markets or prevent loss of business 9 = Key 3 = Part 1 = In Right area 0 = Completely off base | 9 |

(Continued)

| Value | Risk of Commercial Failure | The risk of commercial failure is:<br>9 = Low<br>3 = Medium<br>1 = High<br>0 = Absolute | 5 |
|---|---|---|---|

A total of 10–15 people can be asked to vote on the projects. The scoring is straightforward with the most common score (i.e., mean mode) being adopted. If, for example, 10 people voted for a criteria and there were 6 votes of 3, 2 votes of 9, and 2 votes of 1, then the score for that criteria would be 3. If there is no majority score, then revisit the criteria for that project and explore why there is such a wide spread and see if there is some basic misunderstanding about the project that needs to be clarified. Then revote on that project.

The scoring of the portfolio is also very simple as seen in the table below.

| Criteria | Weight | Project a score | Weight X score for A | Project B score | Weight X score for B |
|---|---|---|---|---|---|
| 1. Achieves | 5 | 9 | 45 | 3 | 15 |
| 2. Feasibility | 3 | 3 | 9 | 3 | 9 |
| 3. Feasibility | 7 | 9 | 63 | 5 | 35 |
| 4. Value | 9 | 3 | 27 | 3 | 27 |
| 5. Value | 5 | 3 | 15 | 1 | 5 |
| Total score | | | 159 | | 91 |

Each project has a total score. You sort the total list of projects (which can be in the hundreds) by their score and see where a natural break exists to draw the line to note those projects being funded and staffed and those projects that will not be funded and staffed.

### Use of the Total Project Scores

Sometimes this weighted approach is called Multifaceted Decision Making. The total score can be stored with the project and used to sequence projects through a function. An interesting benefit of this approach is that if you keep the criteria and weights the same through

(Continued)

(*Continued*)

the year, when a new project arises, you can score it (assuming you use the same people or score it consistently) and then slot this project in terms of relative priority. In some cases, a new project with a high score can bump current projects and move ahead given its higher priority.

### Reapplying this Method for Nonprofit Organizations

This method of using weighted multiple criteria allows organizations of all types to evaluate portfolios of projects and enables them to use qualitative as well as quantitative factors that are critical in assessing sets of projects that are complex and vary widely.

### Lessons Learned

1. Choosing which projects to focus on is a key business decision with long-lasting implications. Givaudan uses a data-based approach to make these decisions in an objective nonbiased manner—and so should you!
2. Having people vote on criteria in their areas of expertise prevents them from being forced to guess on criteria they are really not qualified to assess. In other words, play to people's strengths.
3. Subjective criteria (e.g., fit with strategy) are just as valid and every bit as important as quantitative criteria (e.g., net present value—NPV).
4. Using a group process empowers your people to make important decisions versus only having the "boss" make decisions.
5. Even with the use of data-based techniques, you still also need to apply good human judgment to determine where you draw the go/no-go line for projects in the portfolio. Data-based techniques augment good judgment, not replace it.

Susan W. Watts
Director—Innovation Portfolio Management
Givaudan Flavours Corporation

# How Data-Based Decision Making Can Help Achieve Competing Objectives

### Executives Setting Strategy and Managers Implementing It

When executives set strategy and also establish goals for these strategies using a technique like the OGSM strategic planning method we explained in chapter 1, it helps a great deal to quantify what success looks like in tangible terms. In the OGSM method, G stands for goals and M stands for measures. These are both numeric values that bring clarity to what you are striving to achieve.

What is also very powerful is that managers are then empowered in implementing strategy since data-based decision making provides the freedom to focus on what the detailed data analyses tell them is the most effective plan to accomplish these strategies.

### Sustainable Organizational Capability and Current Business Results

It is pretty straightforward that data provides the measures of the business results as well as quantifying what organizational capability looks like. Data analysis methods also enable you to identify trends for business results, to determine if things are getting better, worse, or staying about the same. Looking at these types of measures gives you overall assessment of your organization's capability to produce these business results.

Analyzing varying types of data also evaluates the variability seen in the results to conclude whether we are being consistent in achieving results.

### Project Goals and Operational Goals

By definition, having quantitative goals for both projects and ongoing operations provides meaningful measures of progress and results. Therefore, data-based decision-making is central to running projects successfully. Assess operations to see if they are within control or are outside control and need attention.

Example project goals are the project milestones being reached on schedule as well as specific quality deliverables and whether they meet expectations of the customers or hit some minimum level of performance such as reducing costs or increasing throughput. Example operational goals could be ongoing production volumes as well as finished product quality measures.

### One Function's Goals and Another Function's Goals

Individual functions (e.g., purchasing, manufacturing, finance) can have measurable goals. Using common measures such as rate of return allows you to compare, for example, projects from all functions and select the function or project that delivers the best rate of return.

One interesting fact is that in today's massive enterprise frameworks, such as enterprise resource planning (ERP) and product lifecycle management (PLM), these sets of business processes cross many functions in a company. As a result, it is important to have quantifiable measures of success that transcend the functions and measure overall enterprise performance on measures such as cycle time, elapsed time, total costs, and net profitability. Therefore data-based decision-making in these contexts use multifunctional measures as well as measures unique to individual functions.

## Top 10 Assessment Questions Regarding Data-Based Decision Making

1. On a 5-point scale (1 = do not support, 3 = support to some extent, 5 = fully support), to what extent does your organization support the use of data (both quantitative and qualitative) to make important decisions?
2. Identify three to five important processes where you are tracking both in-process measures and outcome measures.
3. Identify the data you regularly ask for from your customers regarding their satisfaction with your products and services.
4. Provide examples of documented operational definitions for key types of data that are needed by your organization.

5. What ongoing scorecards, graphs, etc. do you use regularly to monitor the progress of your business results?

6. What types of uncertainty are central to your organization's core mission? How do you measure and manage/mitigate this uncertainty?

7. What do you forecast as a part of running your organization? What overall trends and patterns do you look for? What forecasting techniques or approaches do you use?

8. What surveys do you use regularly inside and outside your organization? What are the biggest problems you have with your surveys? What valuable information do your surveys tell you?

9. Identify at least one important challenge or issue that you believe could be resolved or significantly improved using the right team of people. (Consider using either an affinity diagram or an interrelationship diagraph with this team.)

10. List important decisions where using experts (such as in the Delphi technique) could be very valuable to you.

# APPENDIX E

# Quantitative and Qualitative Analysis Techniques

## Simple Graphs and Measures

Often the best thing you can do with quantitative data is to simply graph it and examine it visually to see what the data is telling you. We will look at a few of the very basic types of charts and graphs. Figure 7E.1 shows a line chart over time (sometimes called a run chart). Run charts show trends for a process over time. This is useful to see what is happening to sales over time—i.e. are things getting better or worse?[12]

These types of simple charts can easily be done using Excel software or many other simple tools.

## Simple Statistics, Probability, and Quantifying Uncertainty[13]

The important thing to know about quantitative data is that there is inherent uncertainty and variation in much of the data that we collect and analyze. For example, we may measure the weight of an

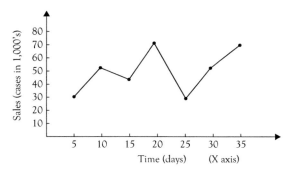

*Figure 7E.1. Run chart.*

individual package (e.g., potato chips) coming off a manufacturing packing line. We may take samples each hour rather than weighing 100% of the packages. For our sample we can calculate the **mean** or **average** weight of a package. This measure of mean is simply adding all the sample observations and dividing by the number of observations in the sample.

**Median** and **Mode** are two other measures of central location that can be useful. Median is defined as value in the middle when the data is arranged in ascending order. Mode is defined as the value that occurs with the greatest frequency or most number of times.

### Examples

Let us look at some common ways that these basic measures are used. If you collect information from your own company databases, representative kinds of data are:[14]

- Employee data
- Production records
- Finished Product Inventory information
- Sales data
- Customer data

There are numerous examples that you could expect with this kind of information. Let's just take a few.

Calculate the average salary for employees by the level they are in the company. The mean, range, and standard deviation would be most helpful to analyze this situation to see if people are being paid equitably.

Calculate the average number of cases of product produced by line by plant and compare these averages to see which lines and plants make the most product.

Calculate the average inventory levels by type of product and by warehouse. This will tell you what product(s) have the most inventory and which warehouses hold the most inventory.

Calculate sales by product and week to see which products are your top selling products and to see which products vary by week (e.g., seasonality).

Calculate the average number of customers that buy each product. Also look at the customer's annual sales to see the relative size of your customers.

## Uncertainty Measures

We all know that the world is full of uncertainty. Therefore, there is inherent random variability in many of the process data that we collect for analysis. In this section we talk about the basic measures of uncertainty and how to use this information.

Probability is the numerical measure of the likelihood that an event will occur. Probability ranges from 0 to 1. A probability of 0.50 means that this event is as likely to occur as it will not occur.

Uncertainty means there is variability if what we are measuring, like the package weight mentioned above. The measures we will work with are **range, variance,** and **standard deviation.** The formulas to calculate these measures are a bit more complex.

- **Range = Largest Value − Smallest Value**
- **Variance = $s^2 = \sum(X_i - \overline{X})^2 / n - 1$**
- **Standard Deviation = $s = \sqrt{s^2}$**

Range is a simple measure of how far apart the smallest and largest observations are. Variance is actually a statistical measure that utilizes all the data. That is, the measure is based on the difference of each observation from the mean. The standard deviation is the square root of the variance which makes that measure a smaller number and in the same units as the original data.

One of the most common analyses that combines both means and standard deviations is called a **confidence interval**. Figure 7E.2 shows the normal distribution bell-shaped curve for sample means ($\overline{X}$). The curve shows approximately 2 (1.96) standard deviations to the right and left of the sample mean ($\overline{X}$). This is the normal variability seen in this sample. Calculating the two end points by using

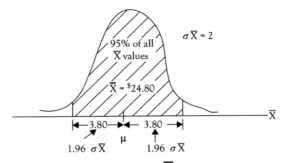

*Figure 7E.2. Sampling distribution of $\overline{X}$ (Restaurant Spendine).*

$\overline{X} \pm 1.96$ s gives you a 95% confidence interval that the true mean falls within this range.

This type of analysis can be very helpful when the inherent variability for your data is significant. For example, let's look at data from a restaurant that shows the amount of money spent by a customer for dinner. As the owner of the restaurant, you will want to know what the average customer will spend for dinner. You can see in Figure 7E.2 that the sample mean is $24.80 with an upper and lower 95% confidence interval of $28.60 to $21.00.

## Examining Trends and Patterns

Often, historical quantitative data is used to learn from and to forecast the future. When a data item is collected over time, such as sales by day or by month for example, it is helpful to examine it to see if there are any underlying trends or seasonal patterns to the data. Figure 7E.3 shows a scatter diagram or trend line with three common scenarios: a positive relationship, a negative relationship, and no apparent relationship.

Two other common and very powerful graphical techniques that are used to look at the relationships in the data are **histograms** and **Pareto charts**. (Both these diagrams can easily be produced using Excel as well as other graphic computer programs.)

Histograms are basically bar charts showing the frequency distribution of the variable being collected. Figure 7E.4 shows a typical histogram for the number of days for completing IT projects as an example.

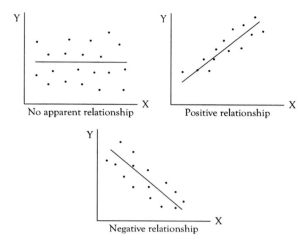

*Figure 7E.3. Scatter diagrams—types of relationships.*

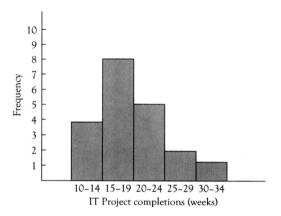

*Figure 7E.4. Histogram for IT project completions.*

The shape of the histogram provides insight as to how the construction time varies. Is it symmetric, that is, is it equally likely to be over and under the mean? In this case, the histogram would tell you that it is more likely to be over the mean. Figure 7E.5 illustrates four different shapes that can be detected using histograms.

Pareto charts are also very useful to visualize the relative frequency or size by using a descending bar graph. Figure 7E.6 illustrates sales by brand data. Here we arranged the bars with the most frequent or largest bar first and then descending from there. This enables us to examine the brand

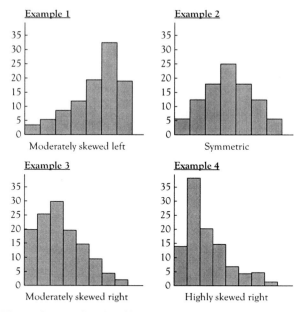

Figure 7E.5. Varying levels of histogram skewness.

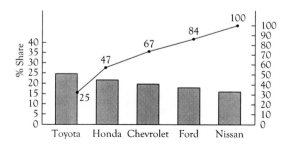

Figure 7E.6. Pareto chart—frequency of sales by brand.

that sells the most so we can focus our marketing efforts, for example, on our largest selling brand. (The Pareto chart is named for Vilfredo Pareto who was an Italian economist.) In this Pareto chart we have also added the optional cumulative frequency line to show the cumulative frequency as you move from left to right on the chart.

## Time Series Forecasting

Forecasting the future is a perilous thing to do. But this is often done in industry every day because there is a business need to predict things like sales, demand for finished product, and inventory levels. Given some important assumptions, there are reasonable methods to forecast. In this section we will show two of the most common type of forecasting techniques for time series data: **moving averages** and **exponential smoothing**.

A key assumption that must be understood is that time series forecasting approaches **only** work when the past is a good predictor of the future. If this assumption is not reasonable for your data, then **do not** use these approaches to forecast. If major changes have been made to the system and/or work processes you are forecasting and you have no idea how this new system/process will behave, it is not wise to use historical data from the previous system/process to predict the future.

**Moving averages,** as the name implies, uses simple averages of historical data to predict a future time period. Table 7E.1 shows the three-month U.S. Treasury Bills rates from 1991 to 2009 that we will use for our moving averages and exponential smoothing examples.[15]

Let's briefly examine the mechanics of how moving averages are done. The number of time periods in the moving average should be selected to reflect the expected cycle that the data exhibits. Since data was first collected in 1991, the first three time periods will be 1991, 1992, and 1993. The total and the average for these three years is recorded next to 1992, which means this is a "centered" moving average. We keep the same pattern until moving averages are made for each year except the first and last year (1991 and 2009) for the three year example. For the seven-year moving average, years 1991, 1992, 1993, 2007, 2008, and 2009 are left blank because of the lack of data to calculate those years.

It is interesting to examine the graph of these moving averages compared against the original data as seen in Figure 7E.7. The seven-year moving

*Table 7E.1.  Three-Month U.S. Treasury Bill Rates*

| Year | Rate | Year | Rate | Year | Rate |
|------|------|------|------|------|------|
| 1991 | 5.38 | 1997 | 5.06 | 2003 | 1.01 |
| 1992 | 3.43 | 1998 | 4.78 | 2004 | 1.37 |
| 1993 | 3.00 | 1999 | 4.64 | 2005 | 3.15 |
| 1994 | 4.25 | 2000 | 5.82 | 2006 | 4.73 |
| 1995 | 5.49 | 2001 | 3.40 | 2007 | 4.36 |
| 1996 | 5.01 | 2002 | 1.61 | 2008 | 1.37 |
|      |      |      |      | 2009 | 0.15 |

| Year | Rate | MA 3-year | MA 7-year |
|------|------|-----------|-----------|
| 1991 | 5.38 | #N/A | #N/A |
| 1992 | 3.43 | 3.94 | #N/A |
| 1993 | 3 | 3.56 | #N/A |
| 1994 | 4.25 | 4.25 | 4.52 |
| 1995 | 5.49 | 4.92 | 4.43 |
| 1996 | 5.01 | 5.19 | 4.60 |
| 1997 | 5.06 | 4.95 | 5.01 |
| 1998 | 4.78 | 4.83 | 4.89 |
| 1999 | 4.64 | 5.08 | 4.33 |
| 2000 | 5.82 | 4.62 | 3.76 |
| 2001 | 3.4 | 3.61 | 3.23 |
| 2002 | 1.61 | 2.01 | 3.00 |
| 2003 | 1.01 | 1.33 | 3.01 |
| 2004 | 1.37 | 1.84 | 2.80 |
| 2005 | 3.15 | 3.08 | 2.51 |
| 2006 | 4.73 | 4.08 | 2.31 |
| 2007 | 4.36 | 3.49 | #N/A |
| 2008 | 1.37 | 1.96 | #N/A |
| 2009 | 0.15 | #N/A | #N/A |

*Figure 7E.7. Moving averages for three-month U.S. treasury bill rate.*

average smoothes out the forecast much more than the three-year moving average (which makes sense since the seven-year average has seven values versus three values for the three-year average). The three-year moving average moves faster and appears to be more responsive to changes in the data.

**Exponential smoothing** is another moving average forecasting model. It is a weighted moving average that takes into account all the previously observed values. The general formula is below.

**$F_i = WY_i + (1-W) F_{i-1}$**

W is the smoothing coefficient or weight. The value of W that gives the best forecast can be calculated but through iteration. That is, use a few values for W and calculate the average forecast accuracy and pick the weight that gives the best results (e.g., smallest forecast error).

The forecast for 1992 using $W = 0.25$ is calculated as $= 0.25 (3.43) + 0.75 (5.38) = 4.89$.

Figure 7E.8 graphs the original data and the two exponentially smoothed forecasts using two different weights (i.e., 0.50 and 0.25). The weight of 0.50 provides a more accurate forecast. In Figure 7E.8 you can see that the $W = 0.50$ line is more responsive and tracks more closely to the original data values.

| Year | Rate | ES (W=.50) | ES (W=.25) |
|------|------|-----------|-----------|
| 1991 | 5.38 | 5.38 | 5.38 |
| 1992 | 3.43 | 4.41 | 4.89 |
| 1993 | 3    | 3.70 | 4.42 |
| 1994 | 4.25 | 3.98 | 4.38 |
| 1995 | 5.49 | 4.73 | 4.66 |
| 1996 | 5.01 | 4.87 | 4.74 |
| 1997 | 5.06 | 4.97 | 4.82 |
| 1998 | 4.78 | 4.87 | 4.81 |
| 1999 | 4.64 | 4.76 | 4.77 |
| 2000 | 5.82 | 5.29 | 5.03 |
| 2001 | 3.4  | 4.34 | 4.62 |
| 2002 | 1.61 | 2.98 | 3.87 |
| 2003 | 1.01 | 1.99 | 3.16 |
| 2004 | 1.37 | 1.68 | 2.71 |
| 2005 | 3.15 | 2.42 | 2.82 |
| 2006 | 4.73 | 3.57 | 3.30 |
| 2007 | 4.36 | 3.97 | 3.56 |
| 2008 | 1.37 | 2.67 | 3.01 |
| 2009 | 0.15 | 1.41 | 2.30 |

*Figure 7E.8. Exponentially smoothed three-month U.S. treasury bill rate.*

# Simple Qualitative Analysis Techniques

So, one example of qualitative data is to examine 50 car purchases and see what frequency or category each purchase is by brand.[16] Figure 7E.9 shows a bar chart showing frequency of sales by brand. This is a useful comparison tool that compares the sales of the brands and quickly illustrates their relative sales. Figure 7E.10 shows a pie chart. It uses the exact same sales data by brand as used in Figure 7E.2 but shows the relative comparison as a visual proportion of a circle or pie.

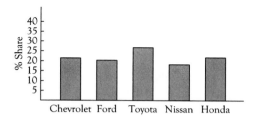

*Figure 7E.9.  Bar chart sales by Brand.*

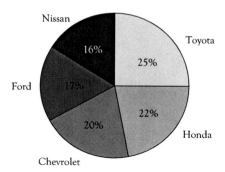

*Figure 7E.10.  Pie chart—sales by brand.*

# Details for Qualitative Analysis Techniques

## Steps to Construct an Affinity Diagram

1. Select the topic or problem statement you want to address. Use a full statement and use neutral terms. Write this sentence on the top of a flip chart or on a large post-it note and put it at the top of the working space on a wall or several flip charts.

2. Explain what brainstorming is and the guidelines you will use. General guidelines normally include:

   a. All ideas are valuable. Evaluating or criticizing ideas at this point is not allowed.

   b. Participants can piggyback or build on the ideas of others.

   c. Participants must wait their turn to add new ideas of build on a previous idea.

3. Use brainstorming to generate ideas or issues around the central problem or topic statement. Each person has some private time to generate as many ideas as they can come up with. Each person writes one idea or issue on a post-it note.

4. Each person has their turn where they put up on a wall all their ideas. As they post the ideas on the wall or flip chart, they read the idea and clarify if there are any questions. Each person is not to sell or advocate for their ideas as they post them. An option is to have each person put one idea up and then allow the next person to put up an idea and continue in this "round robbin" fashion until all the ideas from everyone are posted.

5. Note: Typical affinity diagrams have 40–60 items with those having 100–200 ideas not unusual.

6. In silence, have the group sort the idea post-it notes into related groupings. No verbal discussion is allowed. Post-it notes can be moved from

one group to another by anyone at anytime. This step can take a while. If you have a large number of people participating, you may want to break them into two or three subgroups and give each subgroup some dedicated time for grouping—such as, each subgroup gets 15 minutes and then they sit down and let the next subgroup group, etc. You continue grouping until all items are in a group or by themselves and no additional moves are being made by anyone. An idea all by itself is called a loner or an orphan and it is valid.

7. Now for each grouping, create a **header** cards that describes the overall theme that those ideas or issues are largely about. You must gain consensus of the wording of the header card by the team that it captures the central idea of that grouping. It is acceptable to separate groupings of issues into multiple groupings, each with their own header card. Write the header card on a post-it note in a new color and place it above the grouping it summarizes. Ideally, you should have between five and ten header cards or groupings.

8. Examine the final groupings and header cards. See if they make sense. Find a way to capture and summarize in writing the work you have done.

9. The next step after an affinity diagram is completed depends on the nature of the team and the problem or issue statement they are working on. For example, if the groupings represent key tasks to accomplish the overall objective, then the groupings could be logical categories of work in a work breakdown structure for managing a complex project. However if the groupings represent ideas on how to solve a major problem, then develop plans for how you would implement each grouping's set of ideas.

10. You should have an overall visual of the groupings and their header cards, as well as a written document listing all the ideas and issues by grouping header. Figure 7F.1 illustrates a typical format of an affinity diagram.

## Steps to Construct an Interrelationship Diagraph

1. Recruit the right team to do this work. A diverse team of 4 to 6 people who all have an intimate knowledge of the issues being assessed will produce the best result.

2. Clearly state the issue or problem in a complete sentence. If this statement came from another tool, use the same statement as long as it is clearly understood by all team members. If the statement is newly created with this technique, create a statement that is understood and agreed upon by all team members. Write this problem/issue statement in large letters on a post-it note and put it in the center of your working space (e.g., a wall, butcher paper or flip chart(s)).

3. If the issues have already been identified through an affinity diagram, brainstorming, or another tool then lay out idea/issue cards/post-it notes around the center in a circular fashion leaving room to draw arrows between the factors. Limit the number of items to be analyzed to no more than 50, and 25 cards is more the ideal number. If needed, go through brainstorming to generate a list of relevant factors. In order to avoid confusion, begin with just a few items (e.g., 5–10) and add items one at a time until all items are included.

4. It helps to label or number the issues so you can create a simplified diagram. The problem statement is just another factor in this analysis. Start with factor A or #1 and ask for each pair-wise combination of factors: Is there a cause/influence relationship? If yes, which direction is stronger? An outgoing arrow from a factor indicates that it is a cause on the other factor. If there are relationships in both directions, draw two separate arrows rather than one double-headed arrow.

5. After all the relationships have been identified, count the number of incoming arrows and the number of outgoing arrows for each factor and record that next to each factor. Find the item(s) with the highest number of incoming arrows and the item(s) with the highest number of outgoing arrows.

6. **Outgoing Arrows:** A high number of outgoing arrows indicates an item that is a root cause or key driver. Label this factor as a driver. This is normally the factor that the team addresses first. Identify the next 4–5 highest totals of outgoing arrows and label them as drivers.

7. **Incoming Arrows:** A high number of incoming arrows indicates an item that is a key outcome or result. Find the item with the

highest total of incoming arrows and label this item as a outcome. This could be the real issue (versus the original problem statement).

8. Distribute a legible copy of the diagraph to all team members for their review. Make any changes that seem needed for the team.

9. Produce the final diagraph. Most teams then focus on the key drivers and begin collecting data to verify these are root causes to work on to resolve the problem/issue.

# CHAPTER 8

# Conclusions

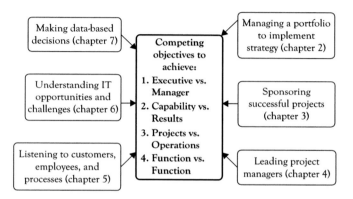

The previous chapters of this book have identified the core 20% of the concepts, techniques, and tools for each subject area, that, if you understand and master them, will deliver 80% of the business benefits possible. These subject areas were carefully selected to enable you and your organization to successfully accomplish the four sets of competing objectives we introduced in chapter 1. Recall those competing objectives are:

1. Executives set strategy and managers implement it.
2. You build organizational capability and deliver bottom-line business results.
3. You achieve project goals and goals for your day to day operations.
4. Achieving functional goals from across your organization.

# Key Learnings

The key learnings we want you to take away from each chapter are listed below.

- Chapter 2—Managing a Portfolio to Implement Strategy:
  A Leadership Team Role
  - Your leadership team is collectively responsible for all the work performed in your organization, so it makes sense to consider each possible project as an investment that you may or may not choose to add to your work portfolio.
  - Portfolio management connects strategy development with implementation through selected projects and other work. It can easily be accomplished through an OGSM and/or scoring model approach.
  - You can identify potential projects and then select and prioritize the right projects to focus on through effective portfolio management.
  - You will accomplish the most overall work in your organization over time if you select fewer projects at one time and then prioritize, charter, resource, and govern them for rapid and careful implementation.
  - Transparent portfolio management with clear criteria for project selection helps simultaneously achieve all four sets of competing objectives when all employees identify potential projects and all projects are evaluated together.

- Chapter 3—Sponsoring Successful Projects
  - The sponsor is the link between the parent organization and the project. As such, sponsors can effectively connect strategy with execution.
  - As an executive sponsor, you can get a tremendous amount of work done through well-run projects even when the project manager does not report directly to you. Sponsors mentor project managers and charter projects to get them off to a good start.

- ○ As a busy executive, there are two or three key behaviors you can perform at each project stage that will greatly help a project manager and increase the probability of project success.
- ○ While a project manager is responsible for planning and controlling a project, as an executive sponsor you have ultimate responsibility to provide resources and ensure results.
- ○ The sponsor and project manager bring such distinct skills to a project that they should always be filled by two different people. While the project manager will be more hands-on, the sponsor will work behind the scenes and with key stakeholders.

- • Chapter 4—Leading Project Managers: The Project Executive's Role
  - ○ A project executive has one or more project managers as direct reports. One of the most impactful tasks you have as a leader is to lead and develop the project managers who are your direct reports.
  - ○ As a project executive, you have both task and coaching responsibilities at each stage in the project life. When you perform these few key duties, you greatly improve both the probability of project success and the development of your direct report project manager.
  - ○ You can increase the probability of project success by continuing to remind the project manager how the project benefits the company.
  - ○ While the project manager has direct responsibility for project results, as the direct supervisor, you share in the responsibility.
  - ○ If the project has a different executive serving as sponsor, you need to work effectively with that person. If you are serving both roles, you need to understand both sets of responsibilities.

- Chapter 5—Listening to Customers, Employees, and Processes: A CPO Role
    - The chief projects officer (CPO) is responsible for how projects are conducted within a company. These responsibilities can include processes, culture, resources, and/or facilitating the leadership team.
    - By listening to your customers and employees and examining your processes, you can make continual improvement in your organization's products and services. You can use this input to help make portfolio decisions.
    - Leadership of customers, employees, and processes is intertwined: by improving one you can improve the others if you understand how they are linked.
    - Leaders need to understand both strategic and tactical issues with customers, employees, and processes to guide the current results and long-term capability improvements desired.
    - Effective CPOs strive to actively engage both stakeholders and employees in a facilitating manner. Enthusiastic buy-in goes a long way when implementing difficult projects.

- Chapter 6—Understanding IT Opportunities and Challenges: A CIO Role
    - Information technology can be a strategic advantage for your business and change your fundamental business model if you know how to apply it to your business.
    - Construct an IT master plan based on your business strategy and your desired future state of using information technologies in your business.
    - Managing your data/information well will provide business flexibility and cost savings.
    - High quality off-the-shelf commercial software is available for most businesses. Choosing the right software vendor

and understanding the total cost of ownership are the challenges you should focus on.

○ Understanding the new business models enabled by the Internet (Web 2.0) is something you need to do before your competitors do.

- Chapter 7—Making Data-Based Decisions: A Responsibility for all Executives
  ○ Decisions are best made with insightful analysis of relevant data.
  ○ Clearly defining the data you intend to collect and obtaining that data in ways to assure you it is free from errors are the highest leverage things you can do to make good data-based decisions.
  ○ Have a balanced scorecard of in-process and outcome measures that you monitor regularly to assess the health of your business and your organization.
  ○ Using team-based qualitative techniques such as an affinity diagram or an interrelationship diagraph can be very powerful in enabling your people to define and solve very complex and important problems.
  ○ Using decision analysis techniques to lay out and assess alternative scenarios will help you make better decisions.

## Going Forward/A Call to Action

We recommend that you look over the key learnings from each chapter and your own results from answering the assessment questions in each chapter and identify the areas of opportunity that have immediate application for your organization and proceed to implement those indicated changes.

We also recommend you identify the three to five areas of opportunity that have strategic and long-lasting change for your organization and charter a project team for each of these areas with the right people to go after and deliver the potential improvements.

We look forward to hearing your success stories from those organizations who have harvested the potential from applying these powerful concepts and techniques presented in this book.

**Dr. Timothy J. Kloppenborg**

kloppenborgt@xavier.edu

**Dr. Laurence J. Laning**

ljlcincy@aol.com

# Notes

## Chapter 1

1. Wikibooks (2010).
2. BusinessDictionary.com (2011).
3. Chinta and Koppenborg (2010).
4. PMBOK® Guide (2008).
5. PMI.org (2011).
6. Kloppenborg, Tesch, and Chinta (2010).
7. Al-Tmeemy, Abdul-Rahman, and Harun (2011); Kloppenborg, Tesch, and Chinta (2010).

## Chapter 2

1. A Guide to the Project Management Body of Knowledge (PMBOK® Guide 4th ed.). (2008).
2. The Standard for Portfolio Management (2nd ed.) (2008).
3. Organizational Project Management Maturity Model (OPM3) (2nd ed.) (2008).
4. An Introduction to PRINCE2™: Managing and Directing Successful Projects (2009).
5. Tom Meyer, retired executive from Procter and Gamble furnished this example.
6. Runge (2010).
7. Devine, Kloppenborg and O'Clock (2010).

## Chapter 3

1. *PMBOK® Guide* (2008), p. 449.
2. *PMBOK® Guide* (2008), p. 25.
3. OGC (2011).
4. Englund and Bucero (2006).
5. Bride (2008).
6. Owens and Sheppeck (2010).
7. Kloppenborg, Manolis, and Tesch (2009).

8. Kloppenborg, Tesch, and Manolis (2011).
9. Tesch, Kloppenborg, and Manolis (2011).
10. Kloppenborg (2012).
11. Cockerell (2008).
12. Kloppenborg (2012).
13. Wikipedia (2011).

# Chapter 4

1. Shriberg and Shriberg (2011), p. 135.
2. A Guide to the Project Management Body of Knowledge (PMBOK® Guide), 4th ed. (Newtown Square, PA: Project Management Institute, 2008), p. 13.
3. A Guide to the Project Management Body of Knowledge (PMBOK® Guide), 4th ed. (Newtown Square, PA: Project Management Institute, 2008), pp. 6–13, 37.
4. PRINCE2:2009—Glossary of Terms, p. 11, http://www.prince-official-site.com/InternationalActivities/Translated_Glossaries_2.aspx, accessed September 16, 2011.
5. A Guide to the Project Management Body of Knowledge (PMBOK® Guide), 4th ed. (Newtown Square, PA: Project Management Institute, 2008), p. 43.
6. *Managing and Directing Successful Projects with PRINCE2*, p. 5, http://www.best-management-practice.com/gempdf/PRINCE2_2009_Overview_Brochure_June2009.pdf, accessed September 16, 2011.
7. Wikipedia, http://en.wikipedia.org/wiki/Agile_management, accessed September 16, 2011.
8. http://www.mountaingoatsoftware.com/scrum/scrummaster, accessed September 16, 2011.
9. Dobson and Leemann, p. 98.
10. Kloppenborg, p. 173.
11. Kloppenborg, p. 15.
12. Kloppenborg, pp. 393–395.
13. Devine, p. 42.
14. Kloppenborg, p. 369.

# Chapter 5

1. Baldrige (2011) and International Organization for Standards (2011).
2. PMBOK® Guide (2008).
3. NDP-Solutions (2011).

4. Evenson (2011).
5. Fleming and Asplund (2007).
6. International Co-operative Alliance (2011).
7. Manning and Curtis (2012).
8. Fleming and Asplund (2007).
9. Fleming and Asplund (2007).
10. Manning and Curtis (2012).
11. Wheeler (2000).
12. Evans and Lindsay (2011).
13. Collier and Evans (2012).
14. Kloppenborg (2012).
15. NDP-Solutions (2011).
16. Evenson (2011).
17. Fleming and Asplund (2007).

# Chapter 6

1. Friedman (2005).
2. Turban and Volonino (2011).
3. Cusumano (2010).
4. Choudhary (2007).
5. October 1958, IBM Journal, Hans Peter Luhn, "A Business Intelligence System."
6. We would like to thank Terry McFadden for the information in this section, which was originally presented (10/03/2008) in the Information Technology class of the Xavier Executive MBA program in Cincinnati, Ohio.
7. Tapscott and Williams (2008).
8. Chesbrough (2003).
9. Huston and Sakkab (2006).
10. Moody (2002).
11. Tapscott and Williams (2008).
12. P&G EA Training Materials (2008).
13. Damsgaard and Karlsbjerg (2010).
14. Yurong, Watson, and Kahm (2010).
15. Twentyman (2009).
16. Information Technology Consulting (2011).
17. Turban and Volonino (2011).
18. Turban and Volonino (2011).
19. Turban and Volonino (2011).
20. Tapscott and Williams (2008).
21. Turban and Volonino (2011).

22. Architecture Forum—Welcome to TOGAF (2011).
23. Architecture Forum—Welcome to TOGAF (2011).
24. Software Standards: SOA and Application Development (2007).
25. Bolton (2010).

# Chapter 7

1. Swanson (1995).
2. Brassard and Ritter (1988).
3. Anderson, Sweeney, and Williams (2006).
4. Swanson (1995).
5. Patel and Riley (2007).
6. Swanson (1995).
7. Brassard, Finn, Ginn, and Ritter (2002).
8. Swanson (1995).
9. Brassard, Finn, Ginn, and Ritter (2002).
10. Chase, Aquilano, and Jacobs (2001).
11. Bardham Ngeru, and Pitts (2011).
12. Anderson (2006).
13. Anderson (2006).
14. Berenson (2012).
15. Berenson (2012).
16. Anderson, Sweeney, and Williams (2006).

# References

(2011). Title of the Web Document: Architecture Forum—Welcome to TOGAF. Retrieved May 16, 2011, from The Open Group: http://www.opengroup.org/togaf/

(2011). Information Technology Consulting. Retrieved from WIKIPEDIA The Free Encyclopedia: http://en.wikipedia.org/wiki/information_technology_consulting.

Al-Tmeemy, S. M., Abdul-Rahman, H., & Harun, Z. (2011). Future criteria for success of building projects in Malaysia. *International Journal of Project Management 29*, 337–348.

*An Introduction to PRINCE2™: Managing and directing Successful Projects.* (2009). London: The Stationary Office.

Andersen, E. S., Birchall, D., Jessen, S. A., & Money, A. H. (2006). Exploring project success. *Baltic Journal of Management 1*(2), 127–147.

Anderson, D. R., Sweeney, D. J., & Williams, T. A. (2006). *Modern business statistics* (2nd ed.). Mason, OH: Thomson South-Western.

Badiru, A. B. (2008). *Triple C model of project management: Communication, cooperation, and coordination.* Boca Raton, FL: CRC Press.

Baldrige Performance Excellence Program (2011). *2011–21012 Criteria for performance excellence.* National Institute of Standards and Technology.

Bardhan, T., Ngeru, J., & Pitts, R. (2011). A delphi-multi-criteria decision making approach in the selection of an enterprise-wide integration strategy: *Proceedings of the European Conference on Information Management & Evaluation*, pp. 24–37.

Berenson, M. L., Levine, D. M., & Krehbiel, T. C. (2012). *Basic business statistics: Concepts and applications* (12th ed.). Upper Saddle River, NJ: Prentice-Hall Inc.

Bolton, V., (August 2010). Downtime prevention through software standardization. *Industrial Maintenance & Plant Operation 71*(7), 22–22.

Brady, T., & Maylor, H. (2010). The improvement paradox in project contexts: A clue to the way forward? *International Journal of Project Management 28*, 787–795.

Brassard, M., Finn, L., Ginn, D., & Ritter, D. (2002). *The six sigma memory jogger II.* Salem, NH: GOAL/QPC.

Brassard, M., & Ritter, D. (1988). *The memory jogger—A pocket guide of tools for continuous improvement.* Methuen, MA: GOAL/QPC.

Bride, D. (2008). Perceptions of the impact of project sponsorship practices on project success. *International Journal of Project Management 26*, 800–809.

BusinessDictionary.com (2011). *Organizational capability*. Retrieved January 31, 2011, from: http://www.businessdictionary.com/definition/organizational-capability.html

Chase, R. B., Aquilano, N. J., & Jacobs, F. R. (2001). *Operations management for competitive advantage*. New York, NY: McGraw-Hill/Irwin.

Chesbrough, H. W. (2003). *Open innovation: The new imperative for creating and profiting from technology*. Cambridge, MA: Harvard Business Press.

Chinta, R., & Kloppenborg, T. J. (2010). Projects and processes for sustainable organizational growth. *SAM Advanced Management Journal 75*(2), 22–28.

Choudhary, V. (Fall 2007). Comparison of software quality under perpetual licensing and software as a service. *Journal of Management Information Systems 24*(2), 141–165.

Cockerell, L. (2008). *Creating magic: 10 common sense leadership strategies from a life at disney*. New York: Doubleday.

Collier, D. A., & Evans, J. R. (2012). *OM³*. South-Western Cengage Learning.

Crawford, J. K. (2004). *Project management roles and responsibilities*. Center for Business Practices.

Crawford, J. K., & Cabanis-Brewin, J. (2006). *Optimizing human capital with a strategic project office: Select, train, measure and reward people for organizational success*. Boca Raton, FL: Auerbach Publications.

Cusumano, M. (April 2010). Technology strategy and management: cloud computing and saas as new computing platforms. *Communications of the ACM 53*(4), 27–29.

Daft, R. L. (2010). *Management* (9th ed.). Mason, OH: Southwestern Cengage Learning.

Damsgaard, J., & Karlsbjerg, J. (August 2010). Seven principles for selecting software packages: *Communications of the ACM 53*(8), 63–71.

Devine, K., Kloppenborg, T. J., & O'Clock, P. (2010, Summer). Project measurement and success: A balanced scorecard approach. *Journal of Healthcare Finance 36*(4), 38–50.

Dobson, M. S., & Leemann, T. (2010). *Creative project management: innovative project options to solve problems on time and under budget*. New York: McGraw-Hill.

Editor, (June 2007). Software standards: SOA and application development: MarketWatch. *Global Round-up 6*(6), 166–166.

Englund, R. L., & Bucero, A. (2006). *Project sponsorship: Achieving management commitment for project success*. San Francisco: Jossey-Bass.

Enoch, C. N., & Labuschagne, L. (2010, July). Project portfolio management: A comparative analysis. *Proceedings Project Management Institute Research and Education Conference,* Washington, DC.

Evanson, R. (2011). *How to design an effective Voice of the Customer (VoC) insights program*. Forester Research, Inc., Cambridge, MA

Fleming, J. H., & Asplund, J. (2007). *Human sigma: Managing the employee-customer encounter*. Gallup Press.

Friedman, T. L. (2005). The world is flat—A brief history of the twenty-first century. New York, NY: Farrar, Straus, and Giroux.

Goodpasture, J. C. (2010). *Project management the agile way: Making it work in the enterprise*. Fort Lauderdale, FL: J. Ross Publishing.

Hossenlopp, R. (2010). *Organizational project management: Linking strategy and projects*. Vienna, VA: Management Concepts.

http://blog.vovici.com/blog/bid/75840/Welcome-to-the-Listening-Post accessed October 25, 2011.

http://en.wikipedia.org/wiki/Learning accessed May 23, 2011.

http://www.npd-solutions.com/voc.html accessed October 25, 2011.

http://www.ogc.gov.uk/user_roles_in_the_toolkit_project_sponsor.asp, accessed May 10, 2011.

Huston, L., & Sakkab, N. (March 2006). Connect and develop: inside procter & gamble's new model for innovation. *Harvard Business Review 84*(3).

Ika, L. A, Diallo, A., & Thuillier, D. (2010). World bank project's critical success factors and their interactions: An empirical investigation. *Proceedings Project Management Institute Research and Education Conference*: July 2010, Washington, DC.

Ika, L. A. (2009). Project success as a topic in project management journals. *Project Management Journal 40*(4), 6–19.

International Co-operative Alliance (2011). http://www.ica.coop/coop/principles.html accessed November 17, 2011.

International Organization for Standards (ISO) (2011). http://www.iso.org/iso/iso_9000_essentials accessed October 26, 2011.

Killen, C. (2010, July). Dynamic capability: Understanding the relationship between project portfolio management capability and competitive advantage. *Proceedings Project Management Institute Research and Education Conference*, Washington, DC.

Kloppenborg, T. J. (2012). *Contemporary Project Management* (2nd ed.). Mason, OH: South-Western Cengage Learning.

Kloppenborg, T. J., Manolis, C., & Tesch D. (2009). Successful sponsor behaviors during project initiation: an empirical investigation. *Journal of Managerial Issues 21*(1) 140–159.

Kloppenborg, T. J., Tesch, D., & Chinta, R. (2010, July). Demographic determinants of project success behaviors. *Proceedings Project Management Institute Research and Education Conference*, Washington, DC.

Kloppenborg, T. J., Tesch, D., & Manolis, C. (2011). Investigation of the sponsor's role in project planning. *Management Research Review 34*(4), 400–416.

Kloppenborg, T. J., Tesch, D., & Chinta, R. (2010, July). Demographic determinants of project success behaviors. *Proceedings, Project Management Institute Research and Education Conference*, Washington, DC.

Levin, G. (2010). *Interpersonal skills for portfolio, program and project managers.* Vienna, VA: Management Concepts.

Luhn, H. P. (1958). A business intelligence system. *IBM Journal of Research & Development 2*(4).

Manning, G., & Curtis, K. (2012). *The art of leadership* (4th ed.). New York: McGraw-Hill Irwin.

McFadden, T. P. (2008). *A discussion of business intelligence.* MBA class presentation at Xavier University at Cincinnati, Ohio.

Moody, G. (July 2002). *Rebel code: Linux and the open source revolution.* Cambridge, MA: Basic Books A Member of the Perseus Books Group.

Muller, R., & Turner, R. (2007). The influence of project managers on project success criteria and project success by type of project. *European Management Journal 25*(4), 298–309.

*Organizational Project Management Maturity Model (OPM3)* (2nd ed.). (2008). Newtown Square, PA: Project Management Institute.

Owens, E. L., & Sheppeck, M. A. (2010). Dimensions of project success enabled by the sponsor/P³M relationship. *Proceedings Project Management Institute Research and Education Conference*: July 2010, Washington, DC.

Patel, V. N., Riley, A. W., (October 2007). Linking data to decision-making: Applying qualitative data analysis methods and software to identify mechanisms for using outcomes data. *The Journal of Behavioral Health Services & Research 34*(4), 459–474.

Picard, D., Page, D., Kierstead, M., & Page, B. (2002). The Black Belt Memory Jogger, Salem, NH, GOAL/QPC.

PMBOK® Guide (2008). A guide to the project management body of knowledge (4th ed.). Newtown Square, PA: Project Management Institute.

PMI.org (2011). *Communities of practice.* Retrieved July 22, 2011, from: http://www.pmi.org/en/Get-Involved/Communities-of-Practice.aspx

Procter & Gamble Enterprise Architecture Competency Training Materials (2008).

Rungi, M. (2010, July). Interdependencies among projects in project portfolio management: A content analysis of techniques. *Proceedings Project Management Institute Research and Education Conference*, Washington, DC.

Shao, J., Muller, R., & Turner, R. (2010). The Program manager's leadership competence and program success: A qualitative study. *Proceedings Project Management Institute Research and Education Conference*: July 2010, Washington, DC.

Shriberg, D., & Shriberg, A. (2011). *Practicing leadership: Principles and applications* (4th ed.). Hoboken, NJ: John Wiley & Sons.

Swanson, R. C. (1995). *The quality improvement handbook*, Delray Beach, Florida, St. Lucie Press.

Tapscott, D., & Williams, A. D. (2008). *WIKINOMICS—How Mass Collaboration Changes Everything (Expanded Edition)*, New York, NY: Penguin Group.

Tesch, D., Kloppenborg, T. J., & Manolis, C. 2011. Stakeholder relationships and project success: an examination of sponsor executing behaviors. *Proceedings Production Operations Management Society 22nd Annual Conference*. April 2011, Reno, NV.

*The Standard for Portfolio Management* (2nd ed.). (2008). Newtown Square, PA: Project Management Institute.

Turban, E., & Volonino, L. (2011). *Information technology for management* (8th ed.). Hoboken, NJ: John Wiley & Sons, Inc.

Twentyman, J. (April 2009). This gun's for hire: SC Magazine: For IT Security Professionals, pp. 30–33.

Useem, M. (2011). *The leader's checklist*. Philadelphia: Wharton Digital Press.

Wang, T. G., Chang, J. Y., Jiang, J. J., & Klein, G. (2011). User advocacy and information system project performance. *International Journal of Project Management 29*, 146–154.

Wheeler, D. J. (2000). *Understanding variation: The key to managing chaos* (2nd ed.). Knoxville, TN: SPC Press.

Wikibooks (2010). *Business strategy/failure of strategy*. Retrieved October 12, 2010, from: http://en.wikibooks.org/wiki/Business_Strategy/Failure_of_Strategy

Yurong, Y., Watson, E., & Kahn, B. K., (July 2010). Application service providers: Market and adoption decisions. *Communications of the ACM 53*(7), 113–117.

Zqikael, O, Levin, G., & Rad P. F. (2008). Top management support – The project friendly organization. *Cost Engineering 50*(9), 22–30.

# Index

A
Affinity diagram, 186, 187
    steps to construct, 211–212
Agile project management, 58, 78
Application software, 163
Architecture global standard,
        171–174
    open *vs.* closed standards, 173–174
    role of standards, 172–173

B
Bandwidth, 165
BI. *See* business intelligence
Big bang transition plan, 148
BPR. *See* Business process
        re-engineering
Broadband, 165
Business intelligence (BI) tools
    ad hoc, 143
    advanced visualization, 143
    analytics, 143
    dashboard, 142
    drillable data, 142
    off-line, 143
    save as excel, 142
    standard reporting, 142
Business process re-engineering
        (BPR), 121

C
Categorical data, 185
Central processing unit (CPU), 164
Change request form, 61
Charter project, 50–56
    example of, 53–56
    milestone schedule, 52, 54
    purposes of, 50
    Ws, Rs, and Cs of, 50–56
Chief information officer (CIO), 7, 137
Chief projects officer (CPO),
        7, 109–110
CIO. *See* chief information officer

Commercial software, basics on
    contracts, 175–176
    customer user groups, 175
Competing objectives
    capability *vs.* results, 3
    executive *vs.* manager, 2–3
    function *vs.* function, 4–5
    projects *vs.* operations, 3–4
Confidence interval, 201
Continuous improvement, 119
CPO. *See* chief projects officer
Customer relationship management
        systems (CRM), 163
Customers, employees, and processes,
        124–125
Customers and stakeholders, 113–116
    customer voices and
        relationships, 116
    developing relationships, 114–115
    ensuring stakeholder satisfaction,
        115–116
    understanding, 113–114

D
Data-based decision making
    competing objectives, 195–196
    global standards, 190
Data-based decisions, 178
Data models, 169
Database management systems
        (DBMS), 167
Database management technology, 142
Databases
    basics of, 167–169
    customer, 168
    logical, 168
Decision analysis, 183–185
    decision alternatives, 183
    decision tree, 184
    expected values, 184
    payoff table, 184
    states of nature, 183

Define, Measure, Analyze, Improve, Control (DMAIC) Model, 122
Delphi technique, 188–189
    standard version of, 189
DMAIC. *See* Define, Measure, Analyze, Improve, Control
Duke energy, challenges, 18–19, 37

E
Elevator pitch, example of, 31
Employee development and teamwork, 117–118
Employee empowerment, 116–117
Employee engagement, 117
Enterprise architecture, 145–146
    methodology, 147
Enterprise resource planning (ERP), 163
Executive leadership team, 17–18
    responsibility of, 17
    role of, 18
Exponential smoothing, 207, 208

G
Givaudan, challenges, 179, 190–194
Global connectivity (LANs and WANs), 166

H
Hardware, 141
    basics of, 164–165
High quality data, collecting, 181–182
Histograms, 202–204

I
In-process measures, 124, 180
Information technology
    architecture and master planning, 145–148
    basics of, 140
    competing objectives, 159–161
Internet, 141–142
    business models enabled by, 143–145
Internet 1.0, 143, 167
Internet 2.0, 143, 167
Interrelationship diagraphs, 187–188
    steps to construct, 212–214

Interviews, 186
ISO 9001:2008, 134–135
    quality principles and leadership responsibilities, 135–136
ISO and Baldrige principles and leadership responsibilities, combined, 112
IT architecture
    defining, 147
    enterprise, 171
IT consultants
    fixed *vs.* variable priced consulting engagements, 152
    reasons organizations hire, 151
    types of, 152

K
KJ Method, 186

L
LAN. *See* local area networks
Leadership team, 6–7
Lean, 120–121
Level of detail and data volumes, 169–170
LINUX, 173
Local area networks (LAN), 166
Logical models, 168

M
Malcolm Baldrige National Quality award, 133–134
Master data, 168–169
Median, 200
Messer, challenges, 100–105
Microsoft Access, 167
Midland Company, challenges, 110–111, 125–129
Milestone, 25
Mode, 200
Moving averages, 205, 206
Multivoting, 189–190

O
Objectives, Goals, Strategies, and Measures (OGSMs), 27–29
    example of, 28
    methodology, 27
    reviews, 27

OGSMs. *See* Objectives, Goals, Strategies, and Measures
Open group architecture framework, 171, 172
Open innovation, business model of, 143–145
  at Goldcorp Inc., 144–145
Operating systems, 163
Operational definition, 182
Outcome measures, 124, 180–181

P
Pareto charts, 202–204
PDCA. *See* Plan Do Check Act
Plan Do Check Act (PDCA) Model, 122
Plus delta chart, 65
PMBOK® Guide, 78
Portfolio, 20, 21
Portfolio management, 20, 21–22
  accomplishing, 26–36
  competing objectives, 41
  components of, 22–26
    governing projects, 25–26
    identifying projects, 22–23
    prioritizing projects, 24
    resourcing projects, 24–25
    selecting projects, 23–24
  definitions of, 20–21
  goal of, 20, 21
  strategy development, 22
Portfolio selection methods, 29
PRINCE2. *See* PRojects IN Controlled Environments
Prioritization matrix, 29
Probability, 201
Process
  analyze and understand, 119
  describe and measure, 118–119
  illustration, 118
  improvement, 119–124
Process improvement teams, 123–124
Project, universality of, 5–6
Project core team, 8
Project executives, 7, 76–77
  responsibilities, 89–100
    closing stage, 99
    executing stage, 96–99
    initiating stage, 94–95

    leveraging benefits, 100
    overarching, 90–94
    planning stage, 95–96
    selecting stage, 94
  sponsor role, 67–68
Project leadership roles, 6–8
Project life cycle, 9–10
Project management
  milestones in, 26
  skills, 5
  success, 8–9
  techniques, 6
Project Management Institute (PMI), 5, 20–21
Project manager responsibilities
  closing stage, 88–89
  executing stage, 85–88
    acquire, develop, and lead project team, 85–86
    delivering results, 87–88
    managing risks and changes, 86
    monitor, control, and report progress, 86–87
  initiating stage, 82
  leveraging benefits, 89
  overarching, 79–81
  planning stage, 82–85
    budget, 84
    communications, 82–83
    schedule, 83–84
    scope, 83
    team, 84–85
  selecting stage, 81
Project managers, 7–8
    competing objectives, 106–107
    definition of, 77–79
Project office exhibit, 127
Project portfolio optimization model, value/risk, 38
Project progress reviews, 36
Project resource assignment, 34
Project risks, 54
Project selection, criteria for, 30
Project selection matrix, 33
Project success, measures, 8–9
  business results achieved, 8–9
  organizational capability improvements, 8–9
  project management success, 8–9

PRojects IN Controlled Environments
(PRINCE2), 21, 78
Project's vital signs, 26

Q
Qualitative data analyses, 185–190
Quantitative data analyses, 182–185
Queries, business intelligence, and
data visualization, 142–143

R
Range, 201
Relational model, 169
Run chart, 199

S
SaaS. See software as a service
SALESFORCE.COM, 140
Scoring models, 29–33
governing projects, 35
identifying projects, 30–31
resourcing and authorizing projects,
34–35
selecting and prioritizing projects,
32–33
ScrumMaster, 78
Simple graphs and measures, 199
Simple qualitative analysis
techniques, 209
bar chart, 209
pie chart, 209
Simple statistics, probability, and
quantifying uncertainty,
199–201
Six Sigma, 120
Software, basics of, 163–164
Software as a service (SaaS), 140
Software programs, 163, 164
Software vendors, dealing with,
149–151
sales representatives, 150–151
software packages, selecting, 150
Software versions and upgrades, 164
Sponsor, 7, 44–46
competing objectives, 71–72
definitions of, 45–46
and project manager, 44

Sponsor responsibilities, 47
closing stage, 62–65
closure, 62–63
knowledge management,
64–65
executing stage, 58–62
communications, 59
quality leadership, 60–62
stakeholder relations, 58
initiating stage, 48–56
charter project, 50–56
mentor project manager,
48–49
leveraging benefits, 65–66
benefits achieved and capability
improvements, 66
overarching stage, 46–47
planning stage, 56–58
ensure planning, 57–58
stakeholder relations,
56–57
selecting stage, 47–48
Stakeholders, 113
Standard deviation, 201
Standards, need for, 10–12
external, 11
fostering creativity through
control, 12
internal, 11
primary benefits of adopting, 11
in terms of size and complexity, 12
Strategic implementation challenges, 1
Strengths, Weaknesses, Opportunities,
and Threats (SWOT) analysis, 23
advantages of, 23
Subject matter experts, 8
Surveys, 185–186
SWOT. See Strengths, Weaknesses,
Opportunities, and Threats
Systems software, 163

T
Telecommunications, 141
basics of, 165–167
Time series forecasting,
204–207
TOGAF, 171

Total quality management (TQM), 110
TQM. *See* total quality management
Transition planning, 149
Transmission Control Protocol/
    Internet Protocol (TCP/IP), 165
Trends and patterns, 202–204
    histograms, 202–204
    Pareto charts, 202–204
    scatter diagram, 203
TriHealth, challenges, 44, 67

U
Uncertainty measures, 201–202

V
Variance, 201

W
WAN. *See* wide area networks
WBS. *See* work breakdown structure
Wide area networks (WAN), 166
Wikinomics, 145
Work breakdown structure (WBS), 83
Work portfolio, 21, 23
World Wide Web, 141

Y
YourEncore, challenges, 139,
    153–159
    accounting functional
        requirements, 156–157
    project plan, 158
    work process flows, 155

# Announcing the Business Expert Press Digital Library

*Concise E-books Business Students Need for Classroom and Research*

This book can also be purchased in an e-book collection by your library as

- a one-time purchase,
- that is owned forever,
- allows for simultaneous readers,
- has no restrictions on printing, and
- can be downloaded as PDFs from within the library community.

Our digital library collections are a great solution to beat the rising cost of textbooks. e-books can be loaded into their course management systems or onto student's e-book readers.

The **Business Expert Press** digital libraries are very affordable, with no obligation to buy in future years. For more information, please visit **www.businessexpertpress.com/librarians**. To set up a trial in the United States, please contact **Adam Chesler** at *adam.chesler@businessexpertpress. com* for all other regions, contact **Nicole Lee** at *nicole.lee@igroupnet.com*.

---

## OTHER TITLES IN OUR SUPPLY AND OPERATIONS MANAGEMENT COLLECTION

### Collection Editor: M. Johnny Rungtusanatham

- *Supply Chain Management and the Impact of Globalization* by James A. Pope
- *Challenges in Supply Chain Planning: The Right Product in the Right Place at the Right Time* by Gerald Feigin
- *Lean Management* by Gene Fliedner
- *Design, Analysis and Optimization of Supply Chains: A System Dynamics Approach* by William R. Killingsworth
- *RFID for the Operations and Supply Chain Professional* by Pamela Zelbst and Victor E. Sower
- *Global Supply Chain Management* by Matt Drake
- *Quality Beyond Continuous Incremental Improvement* by Victor E. Sower and Frank Fair
- *Sustainability Delivered: Designing Socially and Environmentally Responsible Supply Chains* by Madeleine Pullman and Margaret Sauter
- *Supply Chain Risk Management* by David L. Olson
- *Supply Chain Information Technology* by David L. Olson
- *Sustainable Operations and Closed Loop Supply Chains* by Gilvan C. Souza

CPSIA information can be obtained at www.ICGtesting.com
Printed in the USA
BVOW03s1613050913

330222BV00003B/16/P